Fundamentals of Ultimate

James Studarus

Photos:
Stephen Chiang®,
Scobel Wiggins®

Cover Photo:
Rick Collins®

First Edition
Studarus Publishing, Goleta, California

Fundamentals of Ultimate

James Studarus

Published by:
Studarus Publishing
359 Cannon Green #G
Goleta, Ca 93117

Library of Congress Cataloging-in-Publication Data
Studarus, James.
     Fundamentals of ultimate / James Studarus ; photos,
Stephen Chiang, Scobel Wiggins ; cover photos, Rick
Collins. - - 1st ed.
     p. cm.
     LCCN 2003090746
     ISBN 0-9728903-0-0

     1. Flying discs (Game) I. Title.

GV1097.F7S78 2003   796.2
                 QBI03-200171

Cover Photo: Rick Collins©
Scott Johnston, Jam, Catching Disc
Justin Safdie, Death or Glory, Defending

Note from the Author:

Ultimate is an amazing sport that is growing and evolving. This book serves as an instructional aid for all level of players wanting to learn more about the sport. Tom Kennedy (T.K.) and Irv Kalb originally wrote *Ultimate: Fundamentals of the Sport* in 1981. Tom Kennedy is the founder of the Ultimate Players Association (UPA) and Irv Kalb is a member of the historic Columbia Ultimate Frisbee Team. Ultimate was not well known at the time their book was released. Their book taught many about the skills and knowledge necessary to play the sport.

The sport evolved from its very humble beginnings and found its way into communities around the world. Teams and players have become innovative with their styles and strategies. The sport became internationally recognized and enjoyed.

I discussed with T.K. and Irv that it was necessary to update their work into order to keep pace with the evolutions taking place. They agreed, and I took the reigns to develop *Fundamentals of Ultimate*. This book is a follow up to T.K. and Irv's original; however, most of the text and material are new.

This book encompasses many of these developments as well as focusing on the fundamentals necessary to play. Many instincts and decisions can only be learned by playing. This book serves as a guide to aid people in playing and learning more about this sport.

Central to ultimate is mutual respect among its competitors. This book does not go into detail about spirit of the game; however, it should be stressed that ultimate relies upon self refereeing and spirited play. Many players have learned much about themselves and others by regulating their own actions rather than having outsiders referee their actions. Important life lessons are learned from this sport and can be used in day to day life.

I look forward when the day that this book is outdated by innovations and styles that take hold in the future. Until then, I hope you enjoy this book, and it adds to your enjoyment of ultimate.

James Studarus
December, 2002

Foreword
By Tom Kennedy

In 1974 when I first started playing ultimate, there were very few teams in existence. Our group in Santa Barbara played weekly, but only amongst ourselves and simply for the joy of playing. It was more than a year later that we had our first game against another team. That team was from the Los Angeles area and included some more experienced players that had played in college on the East Coast. They showed us some new concepts in play, including our first exposure to a zone defense.

Among those more experienced players was Irv Kalb, who subsequently moved to town and joined our team, the Santa Barbara Condors. While talking strategy with Irv, it became apparent that there was a lack of printed information available on how to play the sport. We decided to write a book oriented to the new player and in 1981, published *Ultimate: Fundamentals of the Sport.*

Since that time the number of people playing ultimate has grown dramatically. The Ultimate Players' Association recently announced over 15,000 members, and that number represents only those that play at the very top level of their respective divisions. The UPA annually sponsors a series of tournaments in North America that recognizes champions in junior boy's and girl's, collegiate men's and women's, open men's and women's, co-ed, and master's divisions. However, the sport has spread even further with leagues for teams at grade schools, junior highs, high schools, collegiate intramural, private companies and cities throughout the world. In addition, almost any community has regular, informal pickup games. The first European Championships were held in 1980 and men's and women's championships have been played every other year since 1982. In 2002, the World Flying Disc Association Club Championships, held in Hawaii, had teams participating from 21 countries.

As the sport has grown so has the sophistication of playing strategies; yet to date, nothing has been published to reflect these advances. Now, with the publication of *Fundamentals of Ultimate*, James Studarus shares individual and team offensive and defensive concepts not previously available in print. The book covers the full spectrum of play, from the basics through advanced strategies that have proven over time to produce champions. It also offers drills, a history of the sport, and interviews and profiles of some of the best ultimate teams and individual male and female players in the world.

James has been in the forefront of the sport for the last decade, first as a key player for the Black Tide, the University of California at Santa Barbara (UCSB) team. During his tenure there he was deeply involved with helping to develop drills and strategies that helped the Black Tide win three consecutive national titles. James joined the Santa Barbara Condors after refining his skills, and this is where he currently plays. His strategic insights and skills on the field have contributed to the winning of two consecutive national championships as well as the most recent world championship.

James knows the game and no matter what level you play, this book will help you to play better.

Tom Kennedy
December, 2002

FOOTWEAR :: APPAREL :: DISCS

**Proud supporters of this book
and ultimate everywhere**

Special Thanks:

Tom Kennedy for encouraging and guiding me through this process.

Irv Kalb for his kindness and willingness to see this project completed.

Jason Seidler for his expertise, knowledge in aiding develop this book happen.

My parents for their understanding and love.

Joe & Marcia Seidler for all their insight and encouragement.

Discraft and Gaia Inc. for their support of this book and the sport of ultimate.

Thank You:

Steve Dugan, Jessica Hellyer, Brandon Steets, Robin Hamilton, Andrea Kelly, Stephen Chiang, Scobel Wiggins, Rick Collins, Will Deaver, Joey Gray, Carsten Steeger, Jeff Richmond, Mike Namkung, Tony Leonardo, Anne-Marie Carey, Steve Mooney, Taka Honda, Aid Mailing, Dan Roddick, Topi Haaramo, Adam Glimme, Mike Weems, Mitch Remba and Corey Sanford.

Fundamentals of Ultimate

Chapter 1
The Basics of Ultimate

Basics of Ultimate
Description of Ultimate
Throwing a Disc
- **Backhand**
- **Forehand**
- **Pivoting**

Catching the Disc

Basics of Ultimate

Ultimate involves a flying disc. The game was first played in the late 1960's as a counter culture sport. It has continued to rise in stature throughout the decades with widespread appeal occurring in the 1990's. Ultimate is usually played on a grass field but can be played on the beach and even indoors. The number of players at a time on a team varies and can change due to number of people available and field size. To initiate an ultimate game all that is needed are players, a disc, a field and endzone markers.

This book focuses on ultimate that is played outdoors on a grass field where teams play seven on a side at a time. Teams may substitute players between points. Players usually wear cleats that give traction; however, running shoes are sometimes worn. Games are usually played to 15; each goal caught is worth one point. Ultimate relies upon self-refereeing and spirit of the game. Players are responsible for their own actions.

Ultimate often involves a great deal of cardiovascular conditioning and muscle strength as one continuously runs up and down a large field. Players should be physically fit before playing competitively in order to avoid stressing or injuring the body. Ultimate can be a great way to get a great physical workout while having much fun.

Description of Ultimate

The Field -- It is a rectangular shape with endzones at each end. A regulation field is 70 yards by 40 yards, with endzones 25 yards deep.

Initiation of Play -- Each point begins with both teams lining up on the front of their respective endzone line. The defense throws ("pulls") the disc to the offense. A regulation game has seven players on the field per team.

Scoring -- Each time the offense completes a pass in the defense's endzone, the offense scores a point. Play is initiated after each score.

70 yds

25 yds

40 yds

Movement of the Disc -- The disc may be advanced in any direction by completing a pass to a teammate. Players may not run with the disc. The person with the disc ("thrower") has ten seconds to throw the disc. The defender guarding the thrower ("marker") counts out the stall count.

Change of possession -- When a pass in not completed

(e.g. out of bounds, drop, block, interception), the defense immediately takes possession of the disc and becomes the offense.

Substitutions -- Players not in the game may replace players in the game only after a score and during an injury timeout.

Non-contact -- No physical contact is allowed between players. Picks and screens are also prohibited. A foul occurs when contact is made.

Fouls -- When a player initiates contact with another player, a foul occurs. When a foul disrupts possession, the play resumes as if the possession was retained. If the player committing the foul disagrees with the foul call, the play is redone.

Self-Refereeing -- Players are responsible for their own foul and line calls. Players resolve their own disputes.

Spirit of the Game -- Ultimate stresses sportsmanship and fair play. Competitive play is encouraged, but never at the expense of respect between players, adherence to the rules, and the basic joy of play.

Throwing a Disc
please note directions are for right-handers*
Backhand Delivery

The most basic delivery is the **backhand** throw. In the backhand delivery, the fist grip is used. Grasp the rim of the disc with the throwing hand. With the thumb

Fist Grip

Series of Elementary Backhand

on top, make a soft fist curling the fingers under the rim. Adjust the thumb and fingers so there is a firm yet comfortable grip with fingertip control. Fingertip control is critical to the precise relaxation of the grip on release, which is needed for accurate throwing.

Stepping Out   (© *Scobel Wiggins*)

The standard backhand is thrown so that the rim of the disc farthest away from the hand is lower than the portion of the rim in the hand. The resulting angle of release, below the horizontal plane, is called **negative angle**. A very common fault of novice throwers is to rotate the palm during the release, causing the disc to turn over sharply to the right. Imagining the rim of the disc farthest from you as slightly heavier than the rim closest to you can help for a stable throw.

Assume a stance with the balls of the feet shoulder-width apart in line with the target. The body should face in a direction perpendicular to the target (ninety degrees to the left), with the weight distributed evenly on both feet. Initiate the throw by swinging the arm across the body, rotating the right shoulder away from the target while shifting most of the weight to the left foot. The upper body rotation, forward arm swing and cocking of the wrist should all begin just as the weight is shifted from the left foot to the right foot. Body rotation is initiated by turning the hips then shoulders to the right. The arm should swing forward in a smooth continuous movement. Once comfortable with the elementary backhand delivery, the thrower should incorporate deliveries most common in ultimate. It is critical to be able to **step out** while throwing in order to evade your defender. Learning to step out while practicing the backhand can greatly enhance your ultimate skills and will be discussed later.

Forehand Delivery

The **forehand** or flick uses the **two-finger grip**. Grasp the disc in the throwing hand with the thumb on top so that the rim of the disc makes contact with the web between the thumb and index finger. While maintaining contact with the web, rotate the disc clockwise until the pad of the middle finger makes full contact with the inside of the rim. Place the index finger alongside the middle finger for support. Pinch the disc with the thumb in such a manner that the grip is firm yet comfortable. The top of the disc may bend slightly under pressure of the thumb.

Face the target with your shoulders square to the target and balls of the feet shoulder width apart. Take a comfortable stance and have a comfort-

Two Finger Grip

able yet firm grip. Novices should initially throw with no excess body movement, simply concentrating on the snap of the wrist. Have your arm parallel with the ground at

Series of Elementary Forehand

Step Out Forehand Series

waist level, elbow slightly away from the body. Hold the disc so that the rim opposite your grip is slightly lower (novices often turn the disc over-this will help). Cock your wrist back and then bring forward with minimal arm movement forward. Try to imagine your forearm hitting an imaginary wall and causing a quick and precise snap. Initially, your receiver should be close so you don't over do your motion, causing the disc to turnover.

This is a difficult throw for novices so: *PRACTICE, PRACTICE, PRACTICE, PRACTICE and PRACTICE*

Once the thrower is comfortable with the flick, stepping out while throwing should be common. The thrower should step out with the right foot; the shoulders should stay relatively square to the target in order to prevent turning the shoulders, causing the disc to turnover.

Pivoting

According to the rules, once a player gains possession of the disc, she must establish a pivot foot. This means that she must keep a part of one foot in contact with a spot on the ground, while her other foot is allowed to move freely. While becoming familiar with ultimate, one should incorporate switching from forehand delivery to backhand delivery. This motion is called **pivoting**. Pivot-

Series of Pivoting from Flick to Backhand

ing is a technique used by the thrower where she rotates on the ball or toe of her pivot foot in order to change her body movement. Pivoting is used to make the transition from one delivery position to another while attempting to elude the defensive marker. The marker is the defensive player guarding the thrower. The pivot is an integral part of the game and must become second nature to the thrower.

A right-handed thrower usually pivots in a counter-clockwise direction. Pivoting allows the thrower to use her range more effectively and is sometimes used solely to fake the marker. Usually the thrower does not want to pivot away from her teammates because she loses sight of the field. The available throws can drastically be altered when one's back is to the action. A proper pivot should keep the throwers eyes on the action in the field while keeping both marker and other defenders off balance.

Catching the Disc
Two-Handed Catch

The most effective and safest way to catch the disc is with two hands. It is a general rule to use 'two hands

Clamping Catch

whenever possible.'

Clamping is the action of bringing the palms of the hands toward the front of the disc, grasping the rim. The receiver uses her hands to grip the rim of the disc in order to complete the catch. The receiver should clamp the front edges of the disc.

Generally, when the disc arrives above the chest, it should be caught with the thumb-down; below the chest, thumb up.

Another type of two-handed catch is the called the **sandwich, clap or pancake catch**. The fingers are extended and the hands contact the disc, one on top and one underneath. The center of the disc is the focal point; where the hands sandwich the plastic.

One-Handed Catch

One-handed catches can be made with the hand

Sandwich Catch

positioned in one of two ways: thumb-up or thumb-down. If the disc is thrown above the chest, it should be caught with the thumb-down; below the

One Hand Clamp Thumb Up

chest, thumb up. Whenever possible, the body should be moved in line with the flight of the disc. The hand is opened with the fingers slightly curled such that it forms a "C" shape. A one handed catch is made by clamping with the thumb on one side and four fingers on the other at the same moment that the disc contacts the palm of the hand.

Chapter 2
Defense

Defensive Strategy
- **Straight Up Mark**
- **Force Forehand**
- **Force Backhand**
- **Force Middle**

Individual Defense

Defensive Strategy

The most common defense is the person to person defense where each defensive player picks an offensive player to guard. The idea behind the person to person defense is for the defensive players to deny the offensive players from receiving the disc from a thrower. There are four general variations of the person to person defense: **straight up, force forehand, force backhand** and **force middle.**

Straight Up Mark

The term straight up refers to the position of the marker guarding the thrower directly up field. If the thrower wants to throw a backhand, the mark will shift over, making the backhand throw very difficult. The defenders downfield must react to the offensive player's movement to either the forehand or backhand side. Sideline support can be very effective in this defense, instructing the marker to shut down a certain side. For example if an offensive player is breaking in toward the forehand (flick) side, the sideline can yell to the marker "NO FORE-HAND! NO FOREHAND!" in an attempt for the marker to stop the throw to the open receiver. The same can be

Straight Up Mark

done to the backhand side by yelling "NO BACKHAND!"

If the offensive team does not have great offensive skills (e.g. pivoting, throwing around the mark), a straight up mark can be effective by eliminating open breaks.

Force Forehand

The second variation of the person to person defense is the force forehand or flick. The idea be-

hind force flick is for the mark to always force in one direction, pushing the disc toward one sideline. Once a thrower is close to the trapped sideline, there is less field to work with and pressure mounts on the offense.

The marker attempts to deny any throws to the backhand side of the field, while the defenders downfield should all be on the forehand side of the offensive players they are guarding. The defense should respect breaks behind the mark but not to be faked out and allow an easy up the line throw.

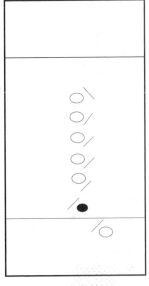

Stack with Flick Mark

Force Flick Mark on Thrower

Offensive teams often attempt to get the disc off the trapped sideline by dumping and swinging the disc to the untrapped sideline (refer to Offense Section for Dump-Swing). Once the disc is off the trapped sideline, there will be more field for the offense to utilize. The defensive player on the dump must try to stop a swing pass if a dump is completed. This is crucial for the defense to keep the disc trapped on the sideline.

Force Backhand

The other variation of the trap defense is force backhand. This defense discourages throws to the fore-hand side of the field. The defenders downfield play on the backhand side of the receivers. Many of the same strategies are utilized with the trap forehand and trap backhand. Both try to limit field space, forcing the disc to one side of the field.

Mark Forcing Backhand

Force Middle

The third variation of person to person defense is force middle or FM. This defense tries to make the offense throw back toward the middle of the field. The mark constantly switches when the disc moves from one sideline to the next. The defense tries to inhibit throws directly down the sideline, forcing the offense to gain yardage while moving the disc horizontally across the field. The concept behind this defense is the disc must travel more yards as it zigzags down the field. With the disc traveling more yards, there will be more opportunities for the defense to get a

Disc on Sideline with FM Mark

block or a turnover to occur.

The defenders downfield must be aware of the changing force. The mark must stop the up-the-line throw and yell which way she is forcing: flick or backhand. When the disc is in the middle of the field, the marker must pick a force and instruct the rest of the team. The sideline support for the defense should echo the call to the rest of the defense. Constant communication is necessary for each defensive player to be on the same page.

Individual Defensive Play
Marking

One of the most important and under appreciated aspects to defensive play is the mark. The mark is the defensive player who guards the thrower. The mark is one individual aspect of the defense; however, it is essential to

making the defensive unit work effectively. The evolution of the mark has changed over the years from marking strictly straight up to today's play of usually forcing a direction (forehand or backhand).

The mark must give the offensive player a disc length between bodies. The mark may not straddle the

Correct Mark Position

thrower's leg or knock the disc out of the thrower's hands.

An effective mark will allow the defensive players to concentrate on guarding the open side, making the defensive unit much more successful. The primary goal of the marker should be to prevent a break the mark pass. Overextending, in order to get a block, is usually not very effective be-

Movement of Mark as Thrower Pivots

cause the marker can be easily faked out of correct position.

The key to successful marking is to keep your balance. The marker should keep her knees bent with the weight of the body on the balls of the feet and the upper body directly over the feet. The marker wants to be able to shuffle her feet, moving left or right along with the thrower

Marker Using Feet   (© *Stephen Chiang*)

while keeping her balance.

The marker must realize if the thrower is left or right handed. Most throwers will release the forehand very low. The marker will want to keep the left hand fairly low (marking a right handed thrower), discouraging a low forehand. The hand on the backhand side should be around waist level discouraging a backhand. The arms of the marker should be extended but not fully. This defender with her arms extended leaves a lot of areas below and above the arms uncovered. A marker with her arms fully extended will not be able to block certain throws. For example, a high backhand released above the marker's shoulder will be very difficult for the marker with her arms fully extended, expecting a throw at a waist level. The marker should keep her arms bent a little with the ability to quickly reach to any position: low, wide or high.

The marker should stay fairly close to the thrower;

however, the marker does not want to foul by hugging the thrower. If the thrower is fouled and the pass is incomplete, she will retain possession of the disc. If the thrower is constantly throwing over the mark, the marker should back up a little in order to have a better chance to discourage this throw. The marker will occasionally want to use their feet to discourage throws. But using the feet to prevent throws often can throw the marker off balance, giving the advantage to the thrower. With good balance, using the feet in certain occasions can be useful.

Another aspect to help marking is to learn the habits of individual throwers. If a thrower constantly uses the high backhand or low forehand, be aware of these habits and mark accordingly. There is not one perfect way to mark so use these fundamentals along with your abilities to help your teammates.

Chapter 3
Offense

Offense
Offensive Strategy - Person to Person
The Thrower
The Receiver

Offense

In simple terms, the offensive team attempts to move the disc down the field so that they can score a goal. No one player can score on her own; each completion involves a thrower and a receiver. Since the only way to move the disc is to complete passes, the offensive team is concerned with creating situations which result in completed passes.

Three basic offensive positions have evolved in the sport of ultimate: handlers, midfielders, and deeps. These designations are loosely based on how often a player in that position handles the disc, and on her typical distance from the thrower.

The **handlers** are the quarterbacks of the offense. As such, they must have a full understanding of all offensive fundamentals and team movement. Additionally, they must have an intimate knowledge of the capabilities of each receiver. Handlers are players who have highly developed throwing skills with the ability to throw many types of passes accurately. They must be able to read the movements of both the offense and defense, and to judge the proper time to throw the correct pass. As a receiver, a handler must be sure-handed. Many types of passes a handler catches are short outlet or **dump passes**, generally not intended to gain significant downfield yardage. Instead,

Handler   *(© Stephen Chiang)*

these passes are intended to change the point of the offensive attack to a more advantageous position on the field, and to renew the stall count.

The **midfielders** are the primary downfield receivers. The function of a midfielder is to get open in positions where he can receive medium length passes. Timing and anticipation are the key qualities for a midfielder. She needs to be able to read the field situation and make timely cuts into the open areas. She also needs to be a competent thrower. When a middle makes a reception, she should feel confident enough about her throwing ability that she can keep the offensive momentum going, rather than waiting for a handler to come by for a dump pass.

The **deeps** are the offensive players positioned farthest downfield. As such, they are used mainly as receivers. A deep is typically on the receiving end of long passes from the handlers or medium length passes from the mid-

Deep Catching Disc *(© Stephen Chiang)*

dles. When she catches a pass, she usually has to wait for the rest of the team to catch up. The deep does not necessarily need to possess outstanding throwing skills, but she is especially effective if she does. The deep should have good speed to run down long passes, and good leaping ability to sky for high throws or floaters.

Before each **pull**, it is customary for a team to designate players to play these positions. Examples of offensive alignments are the "3-2-2" (three handlers, two midfielders, and two deeps), or the 4-2-1 (four handlers, two midfielders, and one deep). The differences vary mainly with the offensive style the team wishes to play and available team personnel.

Offensive Play and the Stack

The offense needs to react to the defense presented quickly. Offensive play begins with the pull. The offense will catch the pull and try to advance the disc before the defense can effectively set up. Against a person to person defense, the offense will usually set up a stack. When the disc is in the middle of the field the stack goes straight down the field with players evenly spaced apart so players will not create **picks**, which are illegal. Two distinct throwing lanes will be created for players to break into. If the disc is off to the side of the field, the stack angles to the opposite rear end zone cone to create throwing lanes. Players will often make diagonal breaks toward the thrower into the throwing lanes and will **clear out** once they see they will not receive the disc. Players will often break in then clear out deep looking for a deep throw on their hard charging defender while si-

Stack

Angled Stack

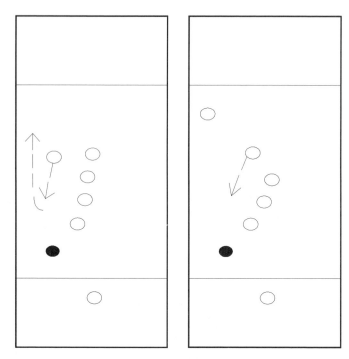

**Breaking In and Clearing Deep
to Open Lane**

multaneously opening up area for a teammate to break in
toward the disc. Often, a dump is set up behind the disc to
aid in case of a high stall count and to open more space for
the players downfield.

Dump/Swing

A fundamental play when faced against the person
to person defense is a two-person play called the dump/
swing, or give and go. The play gets its name because the
thrower "gives" (throws) a short pass to a teammate (the
dump) and immediately "goes" to get open for a return
swing pass. By taking a quick first step, the thrower puts
herself in an advantageous position to receive a return
pass. Even if the return pass is not thrown, the thrower-

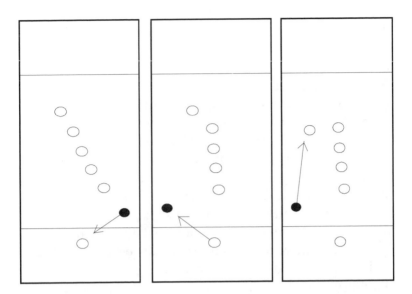

Diagram of Dump Swing and Continuation

turned-receiver starts with a good jump on her defender. If the pass is completed, the angle of attack is changed, forcing the defense to react and cut down different throwing lanes.

Swinging the disc allows the offense many more chances to break the defense down; however defenses like to see long contested swing passes with no yardage gained. A continuation cut from the back of the stack properly timed is necessary to move the disc down the field. This concept is called the "dump, swing, zing" (or downfield pass). If the downfield pass is shut down, another dump/ swing can occur with the same two players or different handlers. The shutdown player will most likely either clear out deep looking for a deep throw or cycle back to the stack, moving players who were in the front of the stack to the back.

When the offense moves the disc down the field using a combination of dump, swing and downfield passes, this type of continual movement is called **flow**. During flow the defense must constantly realign and adjust, allowing an advantage for the offense.

Reading the Field

The thrower must have the ability to 'read' the field. She must first note her position on the field relative to the sidelines and end zones. She must consider the positioning and momentum of all players, which continually changes from moment to moment. The thrower must constantly scan the field watching her receivers and look for open throwing lanes. She should also take into account that receiving skills vary from individual to individual. Another important factor which must always be considered is the direction and speed of the wind.

Timing

Timing is the 'when' of successful passing. Good timing is the ability of the thrower to pass the *(© Scobel Wiggins)*

disc so it arrives at the proper moment for the receiver to make the catch. Passes should be thrown so the receiver can catch them uncontested. Before releasing, the thrower should always establish eye con-

tact with her intended receiver.

During play, most passes thrown are lead passes, which take into account the moving receiver's speed and direction. A well-thrown lead pass is one in which the moving receiver can catch the disc in stride.

Transition from Thrower to Receiver

Once the thrower releases the pass, the marker often has a momentary mental lapse since it is no longer her responsibility to guard the thrower. Good players take advantage of this lapse by taking off quickly after throwing. A quick first step may catch the defender off guard and allow the thrower to get open for a return pass. This quick start is a simple yet extremely important tactic.

Rules of the Thrower

1. Don't be intimidated by the marker.
2. Use peripheral vision
3. Scan the whole field, don't preselect a single receiver
4. Use pivots and fakes to set up the marker
5. Don't telegraph passes
6. Attempt only high-percentage passes
7. Throw the pass at the fastest catchable speed
8. Have the pass arrive in a good position for catching
9. Have the pass arrive at the proper moment for catching
10. Take off quickly after releasing the pass

The Receiver

The offensive team in ultimate is made up of one thrower and six receivers. Therefore, most of the offensive play (over 85%) is as a receiver. The only way to advance the disc during play is to complete passes. Receiving skills are equally as important as throwing skills.

Maneuvering

The receiver has the distinct advantage of being

(© *Stephen Chiang*)

able to dictate her own actions to receive the disc. Pure speed is a great natural asset that can be used to outrun defenders. However, receivers must rely on a variety of tactics including fakes, **cuts**, field awareness and patterns to receive the disc.

The receivers will try to utilize fakes and cuts in order to advance the disc downfield. Fakes can be made with the head, shoulders, eyes or the entire body. In order to be effective the fake must be executed convincingly. The idea is to get the defender off balance and make her react to a supposed move, so the receiver can free herself. However, a fake is only useful when the defender is close enough to be outmaneuvered.

A cut is accomplished by shifting the entire body's weight onto one foot (called the plant foot), turning on the ball of that foot, and pushing off in a new direction. Cuts need to be utilized with fakes in order to free space between the defender and the receiver.

Besides fakes and cuts, receivers utilize field

awareness (or field sense). This is the ability to know where to properly position oneself on the field in order to be in the right place and not be in the wrong area. A receiver often needs to be in a certain area to receive the disc, and the receiver also needs to know where not to be in order to create space for teammates. Field sense takes time to develop, and experienced players usually have a better grasp of field awareness than novices.

Experienced players with good field awareness are always analyzing multiple facets of the field, knowing where the disc is, the direction and positioning of the defensive mark, the thrower's ability, the direction of the wind, location of the open lanes and positioning of the other receivers. All of these variables are constantly changing . Players with good field awareness will be able to analyze these situations quickly and take advantage of any situations that favor the offense. For example if the mark is overplaying the open side of a thrower with good break mark throws, a receiver with good field awareness can re-

Receiver Cutting

ceive an easy throw behind the mark by recognizing what is happening on the field. Some of the best offensive ultimate players are simply crafty and are able to be effective even though they don't have the most overpowering physical attributes.

Often, offensive players will break deep from the front of the stack with the defensive player chasing . The same offensive player will then change direction and cut in toward the disc. This often utilized cut is termed a **buttonhook**. The offensive player will set up the defender by making the defensive

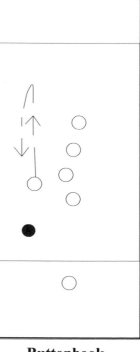

Buttonhook

player sprint deep, then change directions and head toward the thrower, creating an opening for a throw coming back toward the disc.

The same fake and cut can be utilized going deep. The offensive player can sprint in; feeling the defender sprinting, the offensive player can cut deep looking for a deep throw.

An effective cut going deep is termed the **counter**

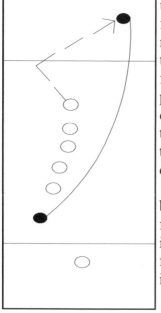

Counter

break. An offensive player breaks deep for a corner of the end zone with a defender closely guarding the receiver. The receiver then cuts to the other corner of the end zone. The defender will usually not be able to react as quickly as the cut occurs, allowing for the receiver to have an advantage of a few steps and much field for the thrower to throw into. The thrower should recognize the counter break early and throw the disc if the receiver has the advantage. The ideal throw should be out in front of the receiver, allowing the receiver to catch the throw in stride.

Reading and Reacting to the Flight of the Disc

Reading and reacting to the disc's flight involves proper positioning. The first rule of positioning is: always move toward the airborne disc and catch it at the earliest possible point. The only exception to this is when the receiver is so free of defenders that she can **milk** the pass by allowing it to float longer with the intention of gaining extra yards.

Understanding the characteristics of the flight is essential to proper positioning. As soon as the pass is re-

(© *Scobel Wiggins*)

Laying Out for the Disc   (© *Tom Kennedy*)

leased, the receiver must immediately calculate the proper
course to follow in order to make the catch at the optimal
moment.

Learning to read the flight is a difficult process and
can only be learned through experience. The key is to
watch the delivery of the pass. The direction of spin, angle
of release and velocity are among the basic elements that
determine the trajectory of the pass. The direction and
speed of the wind must also be taken into consideration,
especially with upside down passes. Assimilation of all
this information allows the receiver to predict the flight
path and judge the best spot for attempting the catch.

Timing is a critical factor on high passes. A high
pass which hangs for a long time is called a **floater**. In order to catch a floater, the receiver must first determine the
proper position and then move there. Just at the right time,
she must leap to make the catch at the peak of her jump. A
well-timed jump and catch for a high throw is called **sky-**

44

ing.

Before any jump, the receiver should evaluate and respect the positioning of other players in the area. Sometimes the receiver must dive or **lay out** to catch a disc that is wide . This action can be spectacular to watch if done properly. The player dives out to receive the disc with one or two hands usually a clamping catch with the thumb on top. Once the catch is made the receiver must maintain possession of the disc as she hits the ground. If she makes the catch and the ground causes her to drop the disc, it is a turnover (even in the endzone).

(© *Scobel Wiggins*)

Chapter 4
Advanced Defense

Finer Points of Forcing
    Straight Up Force, Forehand Force,
    Backhand Force, True Sideline
Individual Positioning
Zone Defenses
Clam Defenses

Finer Points of Forcing
Straight Up

The straight up mark is often effective against teams who throw deep a lot. Most players need to wind up in order to throw deep. A marker forcing straight up can shift to either side in order to make the thrower's deep throw much more difficult, or even eliminate the throw altogether. Teams can often force straight up for a few throws to eliminate a quick huck then switch to a trap or force middle defense (which will be discussed shortly).

There are frailties to a straight up mark. First, the defenders downfield must respect breaks to either the forehand or backhand side of the field. A defender can be easily faked out by biting on a fake by the receiver.

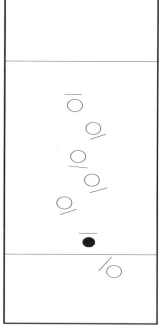

Straight Up Mark

Another problem of the straight up mark is evident when playing against experienced throwers. The throwers can fake the marker out with pivots and pump fakes, allowing the thrower either side to deliver a pass. Even with side-line communication to the defense, experienced throwers should be able to throw to either side effectively. However, at all levels the straight up mark can pressure the offense into turnovers.

Force Forehand

Teams have varying strategies about how exactly to

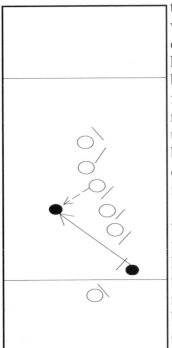

Forehand Mark with Inside Out Throw

trap. Most commonly, the mark will shade a little up field, eliminating any **inside out** forehands, which may travel to the break (unmarked) side of the field. Some teams have their mark denying the dump, forcing up field. The mark may get a block on a dump; however, the defense may get burned on an inside-out up field throw.

Often, defensive teams will force forehand when the offense is going into a strong headwind. A deep forehand throw into the wind is usually much more difficult than a backhand. Forehands are often difficult to grip and release on a windy day, and the defense will want to utilize this advantage. The defense must be careful with left-handed throwers. A team with strong left-handed throwers could foil the force forehand defense into the wind.

The defense must also be careful forcing forehand when playing teams who effectively utilize the hammer. With the disc trapped on the forehand side of the field, there is a lot of field space to throw a hammer into. Hammers thrown correctly can breakdown the defense. The throw will be released over the mark and fly up field to the unguarded side of the field. If completed, the disc will be on the untrapped sideline with much more field to work with.

Trapping sideline can cause large up field gains directly up the line. Hucks down the line or buttonhooks down the line can effectively gain yardage quickly. Trapping is a gamble that can often create either a **block** or an easy score.

Force Backhand

Defenses will often force backhand against teams with very quick and accurate forehands. Force backhand may surprise teams, causing hesitation. Players can quickly release a forehand and often a backhand takes a little longer to release. This slight delay can be enough for a defender to get a block. Another advantage of force backhand is that the offense must usually dump the disc with a short forehand, which can be awkward for the thrower.

With benefits, there are also frailties. A backhand force allows the offense to throw backhands directly down the line. Backhands are usually easier than the forehand to throw deep. A team which ef-

Backhand with Defenders Downfield

fectively **hucks** can take advantage of a force backhand. The defense must be careful when utilizing this defense, especially when the offense is going into the wind. In an upwind downwind game, allowing uncontested backhands down the line can allow the offense an important upwind goal.

Force Middle

During force middle, or FM, the mark is crucial and needs to stop the thrower from throwing down the line. If the mark is broken, the offense can march the disc down the line because the downfield defenders are defending the middle of the field. The defenders downfield should respect breaks behind the mark but not over commit to allow easy throws to the middle of the field.

The benefit of force middle is that the offense must move the disc horizontally to gain yards down the field. As the disc moves back and forth down the field, the defense has many opportunities to get blocks.

The frailties of the defense are that the mark is constantly switched and the defense must continually adjust to the changing mark. With a trap, the defenders always know which side to deny. However, with force middle, the sidelines must echo the force calls so the defense is on the same page. The voices from the sidelines are crucial for FM to be effective.

True Sideline

A final variation of defensive person to person is true sideline. This defense forces the thrower to throw toward the closest sideline, making the offense use the smallest part of the field. This defense is risky because the mark is switched when the disc is swung. The defense must anticipate the switching mark with help from teammates echoing the force call from the sideline. This defense is seldom utilized because it forces defenders on receivers to guard both side of the receivers. However, trapping both

sidelines can stifle teams that swing the disc effectively. *(© Stephen Chiang)*

Individual Defense- Positioning

Correct defensive positioning is essential for becoming a better defensive player and aiding your team. Good defenders who often lack quickness and sheer speed will make up what they lack with good body positioning and field awareness. Defenders should figure out where the receivers want to cut, and then position themselves so that the cut is deterred. Often times defenders will position their bodies in such a way that the offensive player will have the improbable task of running through the defender. The defender must know where she is on the field as well as the mark in order to have proper defensive positioning.

Consider the example of an offensive player very deep downfield. The only legitimate break the offensive player can make is in toward the disc. The defender should be aware of this and front or face guard the offensive player. The defensive player should allow a little head start in toward the disc anticipating the break in toward the open side of the field. Even if the offensive player is faster and quicker, the defender will anticipate the break, thus shutting down a large up field gain.

A good defender should know her limitations, the opponent's strengths and play accordingly. If an offensive player is tall and fast but has poor disc skills, the defender should play behind this offensive player. The tall receiver is forced in toward the disc. The defensive player might give up an uncontested throw to this tall receiver. However, playing behind this player will be more than effec-

tive, making this player use her disc skills to beat the defense. On the other side of the spectrum is an offensive player who has great disc skills and likes to make short breaks close to the disc. The defensive player should most likely front this offensive handler challenging her to go deep.

With an effective mark, the defenders on the receivers have a head start to cuts to the open side. A good defender must constantly be aware of where the disc is and where it may be going next. If the defense is playing force middle, the mark is constantly switching and the open side of the field changes with each swing of the disc. A good defensive player constantly repositions herself, shutting down effective breaks by the offensive player by positioning herself in the lanes the offense wants to cut into. Teammates on the sideline should aid the defenders with the changing mark by yelling up calls (telling their teammates when the disc is in the air), allowing for the defender to get a possible block. The job of the defender should be evaluating where the opponent wants to cut and shut the receiver down with good defensive positioning.

Zone Defense
A zone defense is a type of defense that relies on defensive players guarding certain areas of the field rather than guarding offensive players individually. The concept of zone defense is to deny easy throws downfield. The offense must work the disc around and through the defense with highly contested passes. The zone is often utilized in windy conditions where more throws translates into a greater chance for turnovers. The defenders in the zone must communicate effectively. With effective communication, movement and execution in the zone, the whole of this defense is greater than its individual parts.

The Cup

The first line of defense in the zone is the cup. The cup is usually three people that surround the thrower, making throws downfield very difficult. The standard cup is comprised of two **points** and a **middle-middle** (variations of the cup will be discussed later). The points are on the outside of the cup and the middle-middle is in between the points. When the disc is near a sideline, the point closest to the sideline will be on the mark, forcing the disc back toward the middle of the field. The points are distinguished as the on-point (the person marking) and

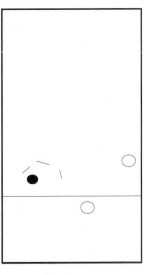

Cup with Handlers

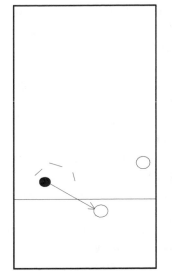

Cup as Disc Moves From Sideline to Sideline

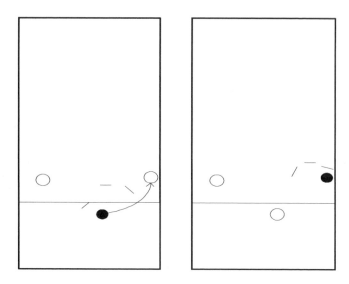

Cup as Disc Moves From Sideline to Sideline

the off-point. The middle-middle in the cup will be positioned to stop throws down the field and the off-point will prevent a swing directly across the field. The thrower will usually be forced to throw around the cup or dump the disc.

The job of the on-point is to establish a mark and force the disc toward the middle-middle and the off-point. When the disc is in the middle of the field, one of the points needs to take initiative and mark the thrower. The on-point must be able to hold her mark in order to not be broken. The cup is useless if the mark is constantly broken, or the disc continuously goes through the cup. The middle-middle and the off-points are allowed to be no closer than three meters from the thrower. If the cup is too loose, large gaps in the cup can be exploited. The cup should be tight (close to the thrower), especially in high winds, yet anticipating where the disc will travel.

When the disc is moved, the job of the cup is to

chase the disc and establish the cup around the new thrower, so the offense must make difficult throws around the cup or lose yards with a dump. The off-point needs to be aware that the disc may be swung and it is her responsibility to run to the other side of the field and mark the thrower. Ideally, the off-point will be able to cut off the swing throw to the far sideline after a dump. Then the cup will reset on the thrower who received the dump with a loss of yards for the offense.

The Wings

Two wings guard the area behind the cup. Their responsibility is to guard offensive midfielders or **poppers** behind the cup. The wings will face the cup directing the cup to shift left or right to help shut down throwing lanes. The two wings are usually designated as the right wing or left wing in order to help positioning so large areas are not left uncovered. The wings are constantly adjusting and taking better defensive position each time the disc is moved or the poppers break. Another responsibility of the wings is during a swing. The wings must anticipate the disc being moved from one sideline to the next. The wing's responsibility is to shut down throws down the line until

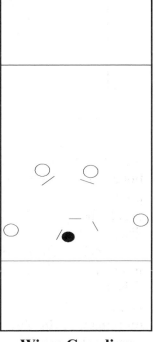

Wings Guarding Poppers Behind the Cup

the cup can catch up with the disc. This is very important so that the offense cannot gain large chunks of yards directly down the sideline.

The Deeps

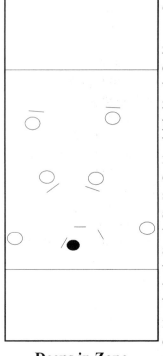

Deeps in Zone

The final position in the zone defense are the deeps. Two deeps designated left and right will guard the deep areas in the zone. The deeps will guard people in their area and direct the wings of offensive players coming in their area. Sometimes the defense will choose to play with a short deep just behind the poppers and a deep-deep. The deeps are usually taller players that will be able to run down and sky for deep throws by the offense. Much of the work done by the deeps is verbal: switching assignments as offensive players filter shallow to deep or vice versa. A general rule is that the deeps do not want an opposing offensive player behind them. Often a deep on defense can be burned for a score by guarding an offensive player close to the disc while another offensive player sneaks deep into the unoccupied area.

Variations of the Zone

The most common type of zone is the 3-2-2 (3 in the cup, 2 wings and 2 deeps). However, there are multiple different types of zones. One simple variation already mentioned is to split the deeps as a short deep and a deep-deep. This defense splits the two deeps, aiding the wings to cover closer to the cup. In this variation, deep throws to the corners of the fields, like the hammer, are more likely to be completed. The defense may accept

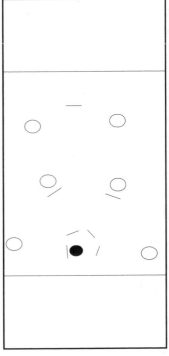

4-2-1 zone

these throws as high risk and encourage the offense to try such throws.

Other variations of the zone include a four person cup. The four person cup establishes two points and two middle-middles. Two wings will be behind the cup with one deep. The four person cup makes it very difficult for the offense to throw directly through the cup downfield. The four person cup can be very intimidating, especially in high winds. Trying to gain yards while four defenders are defending against the throwers every move can be devastating to the offense. However, if the disc does get by the cup, the offense usually will have a numbers advantage and try a fast break down the field.

Another variation of the zone is a 2-3-2 defense. This zone uses two players as the cup with three wings and two deeps. The two in the cup play as on-point and middle- middle, allowing the offense to swing the disc. The defense has an extra wing allowing for an extra defender downfield to cover poppers. Properly played, this defense allows for the offense to swing the disc but discourages passes downfield.

Trapping Zone

Another variation in the zone defense is the trap. This defense will try to push the disc to the sideline and establish a trap, utilizing the sideline as an extra defender.

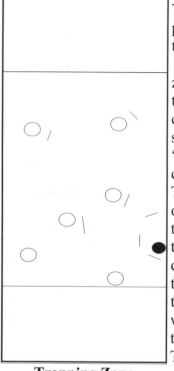

Trapping Zone

The trap is an effective way to pressure the offense into a mistake.

First we will explore the zone trap with the standard three-person cup. The trap occurs when the disc is swung to a sideline. The defense will yell 'trap' as the offensive player receives the disc on the sideline. The wing should be in position on the line to stop the downfield throw and will stay in that position. The on-point that usually does not allow downfield throws will now force toward the sideline. The middle-middle will fill in between the wing and the on-point forming a new cup. The off-point will guard the open area behind the trapping cup. The mark should allow upfield throws toward the middle-middle and the wing and deny throws both off the sideline and dump passes. The deep on the trap line should remain deep and the deep in the far corner can sink in a little to cover area in the middle of the field. The wing on the far sideline can sink toward the middle of the field guarding offensive poppers close to the cup. The thrower will now be trapped on the sideline and will need to break the mark, throw past the cup or complete a short pass inside the cup. If a player does come inside (crash) the cup, the middle-middle will usually try to defend this player. The trap zone allows for long throws directly downfield. The deeps must be aware that a long throw downfield can occur at any instance.

Often the trap will be utilized in a crosswind, enabling the defense to use the force of wind to their advantage. The thrower trapped with a crosswind will need to break the mark into the wind, which can be very difficult. Often the thrower will try to dump the disc in an attempt to swing the disc off the trapped sideline.

A slight variation that can create even more pressure to the trapped offense occurs when the off-point slides over to cover the offensive dump. The thrower now loses an outlet and is forced to create something. More area is left open behind the cup which the off-wing and off-deep need to compensate for.

A 4-2-1 defense can also trap utilizing a four person trap. The trap will consist of the wing, two middles and the on-point marking up field and toward the sideline. The off point, wing and deep must cover much more space than a 3-2-2 trap. The four person trap can be quite formidable in a heavy crosswind. However, if the trap is broken, a numbers advantage will occur for the offense and the cup needs to catch up with the disc and re-establish itself.

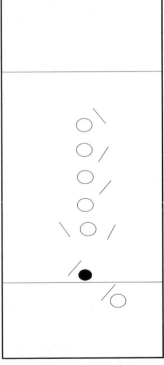

**Clam Split on
Front of Stack**

The Clam

The clam is a defensive strategy that has evolved over the years out of a standard person-to-person defense. The clam can be played many different ways; there is no singular standard clam. The basis of the defense is a switching person-to-person defense that tries to position defenders in very likely throwing areas or lanes. The clam can disrupt set offenses, clogging passing lanes and forcing the offense to improvise. There are many variations of the clam. Most teams will utilize a force forehand while using the clam. Forehands are harder to throw deep and, in general, forehands have a lower completion percentage than backhands. Some teams set up clams with straight up marks as well as forcing one direction.

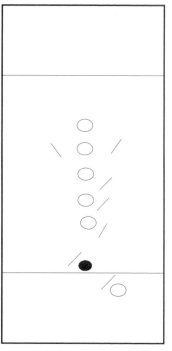

Clam Split on Back of Stack

Simple Clams

An elementary style of clam is referred to as the two-person clam or splitting. The idea behind splitting two defenders is to allow the defenders to complement each other. Often, the defenders of the first two handlers in the stack will split the front two offensive players. The handlers now must contend with a defender either way they cut. The split is usually for one cut, utilized to disrupt the initial cuts of the offense. Once the offensive players cut, the defenders will react and match up person to person. The defenders still must realize the force and position accordingly.

The two-person clam can also be very effective on **shredder breaks** from the back of the stack. Teams can gain many yards by breaking the mark and throwing to a deep cutter from the back of the stack. Just like splitting

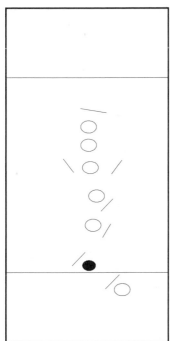

Three Person Clam

the first two in the stack, the last two defenders can decide to split the last two offensive players in the back of the stack. The clam will be for one cut; this first cut will usually always be shut down with good defensive positioning. Once the shredders break, the defenders must match up person-to-person, taking note of the mark's direction. Many teams will utilize the split defensively in the back of the end zone, eliminating the break mark cut from the back of the stack.

A slight variation of the two-person clam in the back of the stack is the three-person clam. The three-person clam utilizes two defenders split shading in toward the disc and a third defender backing the deep area. Often the last offensive player in the stack will break to the open side toward the disc, and the penultimate offensive player breaking in behind the mark. Good positioning of the clam should shut down both of these cuts. With good positioning of the deep defender, the middle player in the stack cannot effectively break deep, and the two breaks toward the disc will be clogged. The deep defender will look to match up person to person on the unguarded offensive player. The clam is once again played to shut down the initial breaks so the offensive cannot rely on their original strategy.

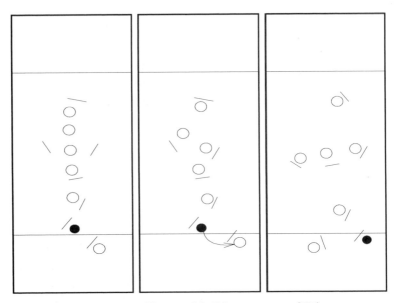

Full Team Clam with Movement of Disc

Full-Team Clam

Simple clams utilize two to three players on the field to create havoc for the offense. More advanced clams utilize the entire defensive squad to shut down the offense's most frequent breaks. In addition, full team clams can remain in effect for more than one throw.

With the mark forcing forehand on a stop disc, the first two defenders in the stack will match up person to person on the first two handlers in the stack, shading toward the open side. In the clam, the marker and the first two defenders in the stack will always guard the three closest people to the disc. If there is a dump positioned behind the disc, one of the two defenders on the handlers will guard the dump.

The four remaining defenders in the back of the stack will surround the offensive players in a formation that resembles a kite or a diamond. One defensive player, usually the third defender in the stack, will front the stack anticipating cuts toward the disc. The fourth and fifth defenders in the stack will split the stack, shading in toward the disc. The defender behind the mark should be aware of hammers and other break the mark throws, like the inside-out forehand. The last defender in the stack will play behind the deepest offensive player. The deepest player should be positioned expecting to defend a long throw.

This clam can be played for one throw and then the defense **scrambles** to person to person once the first pass is completed. However, this defense is most effective if the defense is able to maintain their positioning, trading off offensive players to their teammates. The three defenders closest to the disc will remain on the three offensive players closest to the disc, while the defenders in the back will try to reposition the kite, guarding offensive players that come into their area. The defensive players must be communicating constantly, moving to different areas that are vulnerable. Each defensive player must play their position properly, having faith in their teammates. Offensive players appear to be open; yet passing lanes are clogged, frustrating the offense.

When playing the clam, positions should be assigned to individual's strengths. The first three defenders closest to the disc should all have good marks and a lot of energy to chase the disc and establish a strong mark. The deep defender should be able to cover a lot of ground and be able to sky effectively for long, high throws. The three remaining defenders should be experienced players with good field sense who are effective at switching with teammates.

Maintaining the clam for more than one throw with proper switching can cause major stagnation for the offense. The offense may force what appear to be silly turnovers when facing the clam. A combination of quick decisions and patience must be made by the offense to solve the clam. The clam should be utilized as a part of a team's defensive repertoire. Constantly utilizing this same defense will allow a good offense time to adjust and exploit the defense.

Chapter 5
Advanced Offense

Finer Points of Throwing
      Outside-In, Inside-Out, Hammers,
      Scoobers, Blades
Set plays
Offense Against a Zone
Offense Against the Clam
Styles of Play
Developing a Style

Finer Points

Throwing the disc accurately is a hard enough task in itself; throwing while guarded can be particularly difficult. To play ultimate, the thrower must develop the ability to throw passes around the marker. This requires modi-

Outside-In Release

fying the standard deliveries. Modifications of the stance, arm swing, angle of release, and follow through are almost always necessary.

For the backhand and forehand, the **outside-in** (or positive angle) release is used more frequently than the standard **inside-out** (or negative angle) release. An outside-in release is where the rim away from the hand is higher than the portion of the rim in the hand. The outside-in, or **looper** allows the thrower to more easily curve the pass around the marker. In addition, looper passes tend to hang longer, allowing receivers time to move into proper position to make the catch.

Sometimes throwers utilize an **inside-out** throw while being marked. Instead of looping it around a

Inside-Out Release

High Backhand

marker, a thrower might try to **break the mark**. If the marker were allowing a forehand throw (force flick), a thrower might try to step out and throw a forehand to what normally would be the backhand side of the field. The same can be done with the backhand, by faking the marker (who is marking backhand) to allow a backhand inside out. Both of these throws are usually released low to evade the marker.

A variation of the backhand called the **high release** or high backhand is effective to break the mark. The thrower essentially throws the backhand over the marker's shoulder or arm. The front lip of the high release should stay down to eliminate excess float. This throw is difficult because of the tricky release and minimal spin. The marker usually is expecting a low release to break the mark and a high release can surprise the marker. However, it can be blocked or fly wildly astray, if not executed properly.

Upside Down Deliveries
Hammer

The two finger grip used for the forehand is also used for the hammer. Assume a stance with the balls of the feet shoulder-width apart approximately in line with

Hammer Throw

the target. The direction in which the feet point is up to the individual. The body should face slightly to the right of the target with the weight evenly distributed on both feet.

Using the two-finger grip, bring the throwing arm back so that the disc is above and behind the right shoulder. The disc should be held in a near vertical position. In this position, most of the weight is on the right foot. The upper body rotation, forward arm swing, and cocking of the wrist should all occur just as the weight is shifted to the left foot. The upside down delivery somewhat resembles an overhand throw of a baseball. As with the other deliveries, the snapping of the wrist is critical as it imparts spin that stabilizes the disc in fight.

The disc exhibits more instability than usual while flying upside down. When deciding the angle of release, the thrower must take into account the amount of turn over inherent when the disc flies upside down. Many upside down passes are delivered with a vertical angle of release; others are delivered just past vertical so they are slightly upside down at the moment of release. The flight trajectory can vary. However, for a right handed thrower a hammer thrown moves from left to right. Finally, the disc will helix back to the left if it loses momentum or rotation.

The hammer can be a deadly throw. It can either break down a defense by throwing over it, or it can kill the offensive team with costly turnovers. The hammer is difficult to throw with high and unpredictable winds.

The **scoober** also utilizes a

Scoober Delivery

two-finger grip and is thrown upside down. Unlike the hammer, the scoober is thrown across the opposite shoulder of the throwing arm. It is a flip over the defense. The disc is flipped into the air with a clockwise rotation. The disc will rise then drop. The scoober can be effective in zones to get the disc over the cup. This throw is difficult in heavy winds. The scoober can be released with a more blade-like release or a flatter release depending on how the thrower wants the disc to travel.

Blade

Advanced throwers sometimes throw radically angled, near vertical passes, or **blades**, using either the backhand or forehand delivery. With a blade, the thrower can pass directly over defenders with pinpoint accuracy. The throw needs to be precise because the disc travels directly from one point to another with minimal hang time. The blade usually travels fast and hard. Wind can move a blade drastically because it is not flying flat and is exposed to the wind's power.

Set Plays

Many teams have structured, set plays where players have predetermined cuts and throws to move the disc

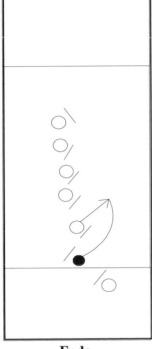

Fade

down the field. The offensive players can gain an advantage by knowing what their teammates will do before it occurs. Some defenses can adjust or anticipate breaks to shut down set plays; however, set plays are often very effective.

Set Plays off a Stopped Disc

Many times the offense is faced with a stop disc and needs to move the disc to establish flow. The defense has the opportunity to set up a force and prepare for the disc to be checked in. A simple play like a give-and-go can be called using a name only the offense knows (e.g. "motion"). Once "motion" is called, the dump knows that she is going to receive the dump pass and swing it back to the original thrower. The original thrower, after receiving the swing pass, can look for a break from the back of the stack now that the attack angles have changed.

Another stop disc play is the fade, in which the first player in the stack fades away from the thrower looking for a looper around the de-

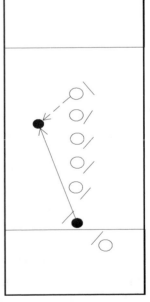

Break Mark to Deep

71

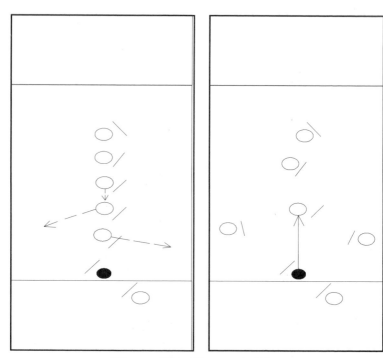

Zipper Play Towards Disc

fender to the open side. This throw is often difficult with limited yardage. The first player in the stack will pinch in after the play has been called to set up space behind her. Then the player will break hard into the area looking for the disc. Once completed the player now with the disc should look downfield for a continue cut in or deep.

A third stop disc play is the break the mark play. An experienced player will call the coded play. The break the mark play usually occurs when a player from the back of the stack will break in behind the mark. The player in front of her into the open side the stack will pinch in to the open side to avoid a pick. The thrower will attempt to break the mark. A break mark throw may be an inside-out, high release, or even an upside-down throw. The offense should adjust and flow after the completion of the pass.

A fourth stop disc play often referred to as the flower or zipper play is initiated by the first player in the stack breaking wide to the open side. Then the second player breaks behind the mark. The third player takes advantage of the newly created space where the first two in the stack were. A simple up-the-gut throw is usually available for yardage up field. Sometimes a little inside-out throw might aid the receiver by placing the disc farther away from the defender.

The reverse zipper is an effective deep stop disc play. It has the last player in the stack breaking in to one side and the second to last player breaking to the other side of the stack. The third player in the stack now breaks deep into the newly formed space. The thrower can throw early letting the receiver run to the disc. The stack can aid the

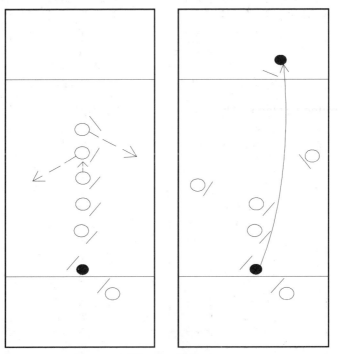

Reverse Zipper Diagram

play by stacking shorter than normal, allowing the thrower more space to throw into.

Set Plays Trap Sideline

Many times the offense will have the disc on the sideline trapped with little field to use. Teams should practice against this defense. One fundamental way to break this defense down is to dump and swing to the first person in the stack, then look for a downfield pass down the far sideline. The dump should fake up the line then back to receive the dump; simultaneously the player at the front of the stack should break laterally behind the mark to receive the swing. Finally, a player from the back of the stack should time her break in once the swing is complete looking for a continuation pass.

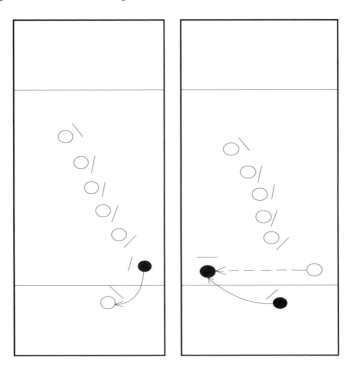

Dump and Swing Trapped Sideline

The dump may also fake receiving the dump pass and break up the line, receiving an up-the-line pass. The new thrower will usually look for a cut in toward the disc from the back of the stack or a long pass to a player breaking deep.

The flower and reverse flower plays often can be utilized against trap sideline. Occasionally, a team will isolate a player in the trap sideline lane. The player in the lane will fake in and go deep or vice-versa looking to fake out her defender and get the disc for significant yardage. The rest of the team should set up a shallow stack away from the trapped sideline, creating space for the isolated receiver. Sometimes a team will isolate two players in the lane. One player cutting in and the other deep. The thrower can throw deep or underneath. If the throw is underneath, the player originally breaking deep can then come back underneath for a continuation.

Plays Off the Pull

The offense will designate a player to catch the pull; a second player will receive the swing pass, near the opposite sideline. The offensive stack will shift to the sideline where the pull was caught; if it was caught in the middle a player will instruct the team to stack left or right.

The swing pass will get the disc to the opposite side of the field as the stack, creating a large lane for the second throw. A third offensive player will be designated to be isolated in this large throwing lane. This player should be very athletic, creating a favorable one-on-one matchup. This player will usually fake deep then cut in to receive a big upfield gain. This same player can fake in and go deep looking for a huck; this play is called a three-deep. If the isolated offensive player breaks in and receives an upfield gain, another player will be designated before the pull to break off the third player, either faking deep, then in, or vice-versa. Players in the stack near the sideline need to maintain their defenders' attention so that no **poaches** can occur. If their defender does leave, the unmarked player should make a break to attract their defender or simply get the disc. Certain teams will maintain a stack on the far sideline during flow to open up space for the receivers.

Before the pull, an offensive strategy needs to be set. Does the offense want to work the disc downfield with consecutive breaks in or look for a deep throw, or use a combination of the two. Such questions need to be answered by looking at playing conditions and team strengths. If a team is going downwind with a serious height and speed mismatch, running a three or four-deep to isolate the mismatch might be a good idea. A team looking to work effectively into the wind might call an isolation buttonhook play to gain large chunks of yardage coming back to the disc. Good judgment needs to be utilized on these throws. The isolation plays work predominantly against a person to person defense However, isolation plays do not necessarily mean players will be wide open; defenses can shut these plays down with very good person to person defense, effective poaches, clam and zone defenses. Occasionally, offensive teams must abandon set plays and try to move the disc downfield without predetermined cuts and throws.

Another type of set play is a **three-person weave** or **dominator**. This offense designates three players to move the disc down the field with swing passes, short downfield passes and dumps. The three players utilize give and goes to move the disc down the field. The offensive players throw the disc and immediately break to receive the disc quickly again, hoping to gain an advantage over their defender. The other four players try to keep their defenders occupied downfield. The dominator can be quite effective as a surprise to a defense. However, this play is both tiring and are predictable to poach against when run consistently.

Every pass has a risk potential or a completion percentage factor. A pass can be classified as high percentage or low percentage depending on its potential for completion. The risk potential is dependent on the situation and varies with the skill level of the individual thrower. A pass which is high percentage for one person may be too risky for someone else. Passes should always feel natural to the thrower and should never be forced. As a general rule, throwers should only attempt high percentage passes.

Endzone Offense

Having an effective endzone offense is crucial for a team. It is extremely frustrating to work the disc the entire length of the field and not be able to score in the last ten yards. The amount of field to work with is limited because of the size of the endzone. Teams must be disciplined and work together in order to score efficiently near the endzone.

When the disc is on the goal line, the offense needs to be very disciplined in order to open up lanes in which to throw. Creating a stack is very important so throwing lanes will open up. An effective endzone offense open up throwing lanes with a stack in the middle of the field. Breaks from the back of the endzone to the front cone is the traditional endzone offense. If the break from the back is not open, the handlers can dump or swing the disc to the other side

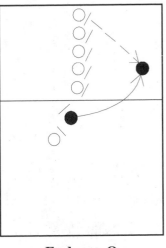

Endzone O

77

of the field and have another break from the back of the end zone to the opposite corner cone. These breaks should be properly timed so that as the handler receives the swing pass the break should be occurring, allowing the thrower an open target.

Moving the disc, patience, timing and opening up throwing lanes are critical in order to have a strong end-zone offense. There is no single correct endzone offense. Teams will often have a designated goal scorer and isolate an area for the goal scorer to break into. The stack will shift toward one sideline in order to open up this space. Some teams also will try to utilize a three-person weave to score a goal. Teamwork is crucial when on the endzone.

Offense Against a Zone

Playing against a zone defense offers challenges quite different from playing against a person to person de-fense. The positioning of defensive players is more clearly defined in a zone. An offense can take advantage of this predictability by playing smart. The first step is to deter-mine which zone defense is being played (3-2-2, 4-2-1, see zone section). Once the type of zone has been determined,

(© *Scobel Wiggins*)

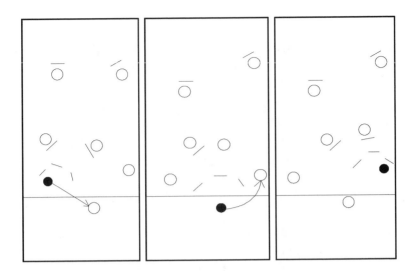

Zone O with Disc Swinging

the location of the seams and holes become apparent. Recognizing the alignment of the zone allows the offense to choose its most effective distribution and placement of the handlers, midfielders and deeps.

While deterring substantial downfield gains, zone defenses usually put little pressure on short lateral passes. Offensive teams can take advantage of this by always positioning a handler to receive a dump pass. However, when throwing downfield, passes should be thrown down a seam, or into a hole, in the defense.

When playing in a midfield or deep position, receivers often get the feeling of being unguarded since there is no individual coverage. Different techniques for getting truly open must be employed. The sharp cuts used against a person to person defense are not as effective. Because defenders in a zone usually face the thrower, the most effective movement a downfield receiver can make is to approach the areas open to the thrower from the defender's blind side. Knowing where the holes and seams are allows the receivers to make their most effective movements.

The offense will usually have three handlers swing the disc from one sideline, to the middle of the field, then to the other sideline. This causes the zone to spread out and cover more area. Two poppers will try to receive the disc between the seams of the cup. The poppers move constantly looking for seams to exploit. The poppers can come inside the cup if the cup is too loose in order to gain yards. Two deeps run the sidelines, attempting to spread the defense and receive up-the-line throws. The deeps will break in when the disc comes to their sideline, looking for an up the line gain. The second deep can break diagonally deep looking for a deep throw into the newly created deep area. The deep position is often unheralded because they don't touch the disc as much as the handlers or poppers; but, they are vital to spread out the zone.

Variations of the 3-2-2 offense can be changed to two handlers, two wings, two poppers, and one deep. Or it can be adjusted to four handlers, two poppers and one deep. These last two offenses are similar although the wings in the 2-2-2-1 look for more upfield gains. The 4-2-1 look can be helpful with short, quick swing passes in high winds or against a formidable four-person zone cup.

The purposeful overloading of a particular zone is sometimes utilized, contrary to the concept of spreading the zone defense. As mentioned earlier, a defender in a zone finds it difficult to cover more than one receiver. A clever thrower can read the situation by watching the defender in the overloaded zone. If the defender shifts to cover one receiver, the other receiver becomes open. Care must be taken to watch for defenders who try to "cheat over" to help defend the overload.

Offense Against the Clam

A team might throw a clam defense for one or more throws. The offense needs to recognize this because

poaching is prevalent. Moving the disc is crucial to open throwing lanes. Dumping and swinging is always a sound method. If the clam is for a short number of throws, by the time the dump and swing go off, a person to person defense will appear and flowing the disc down the field will be the goal. If the clam persists, a zone offense like a 3-2-2 can be effective as well. In general, patience while moving the disc must be utilized to spread the clam and expose lanes.

Styles of Play

There exist many theories on the best way to run the offense. These theories cover the whole spectrum from a controlled short-pass offense to the wide-open long bomb, or huck, offense.

81

The control offense is based upon the short, accurate pass - each being a high percentage pass, usually fifteen yards or less. The key factors involved in this style are consistency and patience, as a great number of passes need to be completed in order to score. It takes a great deal of self-control on the part of each offensive player to restrict the pass selection to short range passes. However, since each pass has such a high percentage of completion and the offense is consistent and patient, it will usually score.

At the other end of the spectrum is the huck offense. The basic idea is to move the disc into position so that a long pass may be attempted during most possessions. The theory is that, if a team has fast, tall receivers who can jump and catch well, it can count on completing these passes better than fifty percent of the time. The theory goes on to state that even if the pass is not completed, the opposition must then move the disc the full length of the field to score.

Somewhere between the control and huck offense is the flow offense. It is not restricted to one length of pass and actually encourages a good mix. As described earlier, the flow depends on uninterrupted movement of the disc. The basic idea behind the flow is to complete passes in rapid succession by having receivers make proper cuts in sequence while the disc is moving downfield. This style is difficult because it relies heavily on precise timing. Each time a pass is caught, the thrower pivots quickly, anticipating the next receiver's break, and vice versa. The receivers must time their cuts so that they get open just after the previous pass is completed.

A unique style of play has evolved in Europe that has become an effective way for offenses to play. Most defensive players have their backs to the thrower, face guarding the receivers downfield. The European strategy takes advantage of the fact that the defender is not looking at the thrower while the receiver is. The thrower will simply throw the disc to space and let the receiver go to the disc. Most offenses let the receiver break into space. However, this European style allows the thrower to throw to space. The receiver is expected to adjust before the defender is able to react.

European teams often isolate two receivers in the stack with two dumps and two receivers split very deep. Space is now opened up in the middle of the field for the thrower to throw into. For example, on a force forehand, the thrower will release the hammer to space before the receiver breaks. The receiver reacts and will hopefully catch the disc before the defender knows what happened.

Weather conditions and the defense often determines styles of play. A very windy game can be played with a lot of zone defense with short throws and limited running on offense. The same two teams in a game with no breeze can see wide-open person to person defenses with plenty of running and long throws. Teams should be able to use a variety of styles of play depending on the conditions and opposing defenses.

Developing a Style

Combining the tactics described here, teams can develop their own system. This depends on many factors. Experience, speed, height, and competence of each individual team member has significant influence on the offensive style. The amount of practice time available also greatly affects this choice. In order to develop a team offense, many hours need to be spent practicing together. Each player develops personal habits of movement. Only through constant practice can players take advantage of being familiar with their teammates' movements.

Chapter 6
Drills

Three Person Marker Drill

This is a simple drill that works on the fundamentals of throwing while being guarded. It is a good drill for both the thrower and marker. One person has the disc and is throwing to a stationary receiver ten yards away. The marker marks straight up, trying to deny throws to the stationary receiver. The marker checks the disc in and starts stalling at count six. The thrower must pivot and fake the marker in order to complete the pass. Overhead throws such as hammers and scoobers are not allowed. Floating and/or weak passes are discouraged. Once the thrower completes the throw, she runs to mark the receiver, and the original marker now becomes the new receiver. This is a great drill to work on both your mark, as well as breaking the mark.

Endzone Drill

This is another team drill that works on endzone offense. There is a line in the back of the end zone and one in the front of the end zone. A player from the back of the endzone breaks to the front corner cone when the

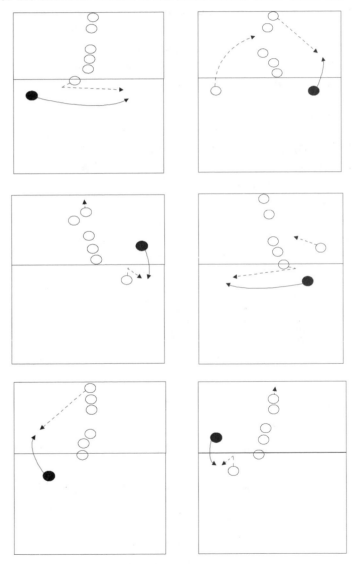

disc is swung to a handler from the front line. The handler throws into the goal to the breaking receiver. The same handler receives a dump pass from the receiver who just caught the disc in the goal, then swings the disc to a handler breaking out of the front of the stack. Another break from the back should be timed so that as the swing is caught, the receiver initiates the cut. Players should rotate to the other line after making their cuts. This drill works on dumping and swinging the disc as well as properly timing breaks from the back of the endzone.

Trap Sideline Drill

Teams must often face a trapping person to person defense with the disc on the sideline. This drill works on both offensive and defensive aspects. The thrower has the disc on the sideline, being trapped by a marker. This drill works on the dump breaking either up the line or back for a dump. There should be an unguarded offensive player deep in the stack as well as a shallow offensive in the stack

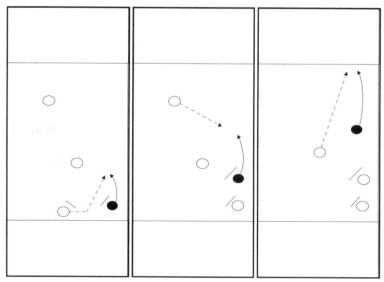

Option with Dump Up Line

also unguarded. The dump player should be guarded.

The dump has options. She can break up the line and receive an up the line pass. Then the player in the back of the stack breaks in for an up the line throw, fol-lowed by the shallow player in the stack breaking deep, then in, for the third throw. Or the shallow player in the stack can simply break deep for a long throw.

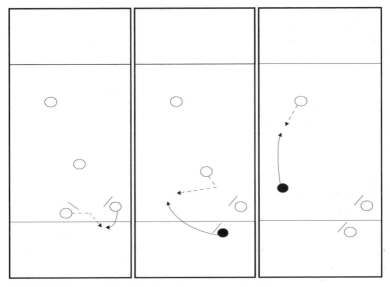

Option with Dump, Swing

The other option has the dump faking up the line and receiving a dump pass. Once the dump is received, the front player in the stack breaks for a swing behind the mark. The defender on the dump should try to prevent the swing throw from occurring. Once the swing goes off to the front player in the stack, the deep should break in to receive an up field gain behind the mark. The drill should be run with the disc trapped on both the forehand and backhand sides of the field. This drill works on beating a sideline trap.

Box Drill-Four Corners

     This is a simple offensive drill that works on timing and lead passes. Players set up in all four corners about 20 yards apart. A player breaks from an adjacent corner looking for a lead pass from the corner where she started. Once the pass is received the receiver in the closest line breaks toward the next corner looking for a lead pass. If the drill is run clockwise, the throwers should be utilizing forehands. Counterclockwise, backhands should be used. Receivers can set up breaks by breaking out of the box, then in to cut off the angle in order to make the throw and catch a little easier. This drill is good on windy days because the throwers must throw with the wind blowing in all directions.

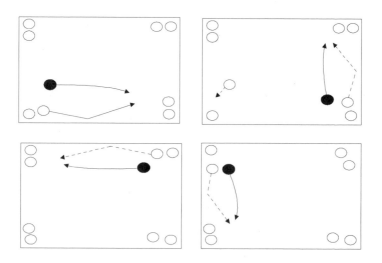

Straight Ahead Drill

     This is a drill that works on receivers running directly at a thrower and catching a pass. Set up a line of receivers facing one thrower. The thrower releases the disc directly at the oncoming receiver. The receiver runs to the disc and catches the disc; then the receiver throws the disc back to the original thrower. She then runs to the back of the line, clearing space for the next receiver to break in toward the thrower. A slight variation is for the receivers to initiate their break deep then buttonhook toward the thrower to mimic a real game comeback cut. An entire team can do this with multiple lines of receivers and throwers. A team of twenty can split up with four throwers and four lines of four receivers. The receivers can rotate to the next line in order to catch passes from all the throwers. This drill can tire out the receivers, which will mimic a game situation.

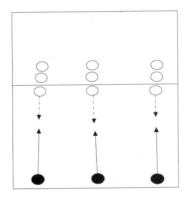 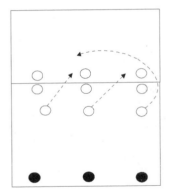

Counter Drill

This drill works on receivers making counter breaks and throwers putting the disc out in front of the receiver. The receiver will break deep toward the far corner of the end zone, then counter toward the opposite corner of the endzone. The thrower should throw the pass as soon as the receiver counters, allowing the disc to be out in front of

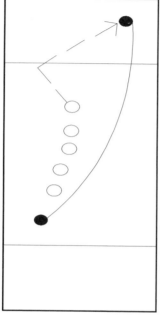

the receiver so the receiver can catch the disc in stride. If the receiver breaks deep looking for a forehand then counters for a backhand, the receiver should be conscious of the sideline. The receiver should break for the backhand with a defender charging hard defending against the potential forehand. This is an advanced drill that works on proper deep breaks and solid deep throws. Throwers and receivers should start this drill with accurate, shorter, throws then advance to longer and deeper breaks.

45 Degree Break Drill

Set up two people facing each other about 25 yards apart. Teammates will be behind each of the front people in line. The first person in one of the lines initiates the drill by breaking in at a 45 degree cut toward the thrower. The thrower throws the disc to space in front of the receiver. As soon as the thrower releases the disc, she breaks at a 45 degree angle toward the open space. Once the receiver catches the disc, she should clear out to the back of the opposite line with disc in hand. The drill should switch directions after multiple throws to work on the forehand and backhand throws. The thrower should work on throwing to the outside of the field with the forehand or backhand. Once comfortable with these throws, the thrower can work on throwing inside-out throws. This drill works on cutting

at full speed and throwing lead passes. This is a great drill
for all levels of play.

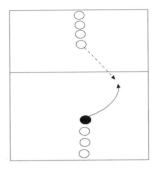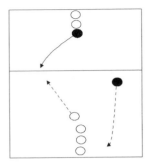

45 Degree Break Drill with Mark

A slight variation of the drill just described includes having a marker defending the thrower. The thrower must
break the mark to complete the throw to the receiver cutting from the opposite line. The thrower should throw an
inside-out throw or a break mark throw around the marker.
Hammers or scoobers are not encouraged in this drill. This
drill works on pivoting, moving the marker and throwing
with a marker on the thrower. An effective throw should
be early in order to hit the cutter as soon as she initiates the
cut. Once the thrower releases the disc, she should initiate

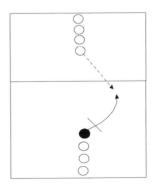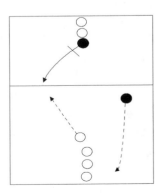

a 45 degree cut in order to receive a pass from the other line. Once the receiver catches the disc, she should clear out to the back of the opposite line. A simple rotation of marker to thrower to receiver allows for this drill to run smoothly.

Lead Pass Drill

This drill works on throwers leading receivers breaking away downfield. The thrower should be close to a sideline facing downfield. The receiver runs from shallow to deep, anticipating a lead pass ahead into the space downfield. The thrower can throw a short, medium or deep pass depending on skill, wind and desired distance. The thrower should throw early and let the receiver run onto the disc in stride. The disc should not float too much, forcing the receiver to wait for the disc. This drill should be done on the fore-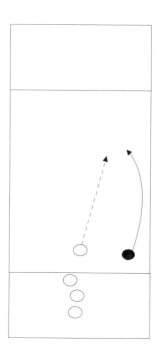hand and backhand sides of the field.

Kill Drill

This drill involves two people. One person is the thrower and the other person is the receiver (or the one being killed). The receiver breaks to one side of the thrower for about 5 steps and receives a pass. The receiver plants and quickly tosses the disc back to the stationary thrower. The receiver then breaks in the opposite direction for about 5 steps receives a pass and quickly tosses it back. This drill works on conditioning and catching the disc while tired. Teams can start by doing the drill for 30 seconds then work their way to a minute with multiple repetitions.

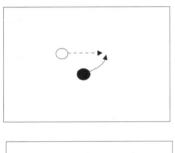

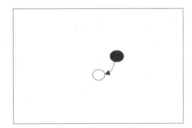

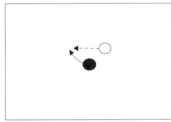

Chapter 7
History, Profiles &
Interviews

Ultimate is a global sport played in over forty countries. Ultimate started as a simple game with no referees that relied upon spirit and sportsmanship among its competitors. In thirty years, the sport has grown in prominence and stature all over the globe while staying in touch with its innocent roots. Ultimate is now played throughout the world at casual pickup games to world-class championships.

Discs were first thrown in the late 1800's when New England college students hurled baking dishes from the Frisbie Baking Company of Connecticut. Discs became part of popular culture with Wham-O's discs in the mid 1960's. Ultimate followed a few years later when Columbia High School in Maplewood, New Jersey began playing a form of field disc 1967. Joel Silver started the first team and played the first official game in 1968 in New Jersey.

Graduates of the Columbia High School team developed college teams. In 1972, Rutgers and Princeton played the first collegiate game. The first official tournament was held in 1975 at Yale with eight teams participating. This tournament was expanded and renamed the National Ultimate Championships. The tournament used spirit of the game to allow the players to self-referee. Rutgers dominated the first few years of the tournament. The Santa Barbara Condors won the tournament in 1977, proving that ultimate was a mainstay on both coasts. In 1979, the Ultimate Players Association (UPA) was formed with

Tom Kennedy becoming the first director. This same year, the first UPA Nationals were held in Pennsylvania. Two years later, a women's division was added to UPA Nationals. Ultimate leagues began springing up in cities and colleges throughout the US.

Ultimate spread as a global sport with players from all over the world participating. In 1980, the first European Ultimate Championships were held in Paris. Three years later, the first World Championships were held in Sweden with teams from Europe and the United States participating in this historic event. A year later, Japan participated in the World Championships; cementing ultimate's global trend. Also in 1984, the first UPA College Nationals were held; three years later the women's division was added. College ultimate has grown tremendously in the United States and has become very important for the sport's growth and level of ability.

Ultimate has risen in stature with the emergence of teams that push the games limits and boundaries. New York New York dominated men's ultimate during the early 1990's, elevating the sport to a new level with athleticism and team strategy. On New York's heels, Boston's Death or Glory again raised the level of play with their dominance in the late 90's. The Lady Condors elevated the women's game during the 1980's, winning numerous World and National Championships. Boston's Lady Godiva has established a new threshold of how to play the game with their athleticism, disc skills and execution. These teams have inspired players across the globe to perform better and take the game to new heights.

Tremendous strides have been taken since its humble beginnings. Tournaments all over the world still rely upon spirit of the game, bringing players to judge their own actions, balancing competition with fairness. Ultimate has not achieved huge commercial success, which causes many to raise questions about the sport's stature. Yet, ultimate has persevered, continuing to grow and evolve as an exciting and fun sport. Players from high school students to executives all over this world play this sport. Many more will learn and teach this sport as its appeal increases. As strikes, scandals and allegations mar many sports, ultimate has remained with its roots, playing with spirit and for the enjoyment of the game.

Profile: Lady Godiva

Since its inception in 1987, Boston's Lady Godiva has been an elite women's ultimate team. In its first year, Lady Godiva reached the finals of Nationals but lost to the then dominant Santa Barbara Condors. Lady Godiva went head to head against another Boston team, the Smithereens, and won its first National championship in 1988.

The early 90's were dominated by a rivalry with the San Francisco team, the Maine-iacs. In 1991 Godiva went on to defeat the Maine-iacs to take their second National Title. The next two years, the rivalry continued as Godiva fought with the Maine-iacs for the National Championship but came up short in 1992 and 1993, losing in the finals both years. 1994 was another turnover year with newcomers and new leadership the team didn't advance further than the semis at Nationals.

In 1995, the team had stabilized and came into the 1995 Nationals with something to prove. Lady Godiva went on to win the next 4 Nation-

(© Stephen Chiang)

als Championships, 1995 through 1998 with their consistent, patient and efficient offense along with a stifling defense.

In 1998 Lady Godiva represented USA as team USA in the International Worlds Competition and won the Worlds Ultimate Championship. Lady Godiva won the 2000, 2001 and 2002 UPA National Championships, solidifying their dominance in women's ultimate. Godiva is committed to winning, and are raising the level of play in women's ultimate to a higher level.

(© Stephen Chiang)

(© Rick Collins)

98

Profile: New York New York

New York New York dominated open ultimate during the early '90's. This team was the first true dynasty of the open division. Athleticism, hard nosed play and a will to never lose drove this team to the top of the sport.
Kenny Dobyns epitomized this style of play. The stocky and powerful Dobyns could run, jump and throw past opponents on the way to victory. With the aid of 6'7" teammate Dennis 'Cribber' Warsen, the two became a headache for opponents as they caught or threw numerous goals.

New York New York was much deeper than two stars. With an array zone defenses and tight man defense, New York routinely shut down opposing offenses. Their wide open, free form offense was efficient and effective. Players like Billy Rodriguez, Pat King, Jonathan Gewirtz, and Dave Babkow combined disc skills, experience and athleticism to excel.

The team possessed tremendous emotion and created tremendous passion from opponents and the sidelines.

(© Jost Armbruster)

The New York Times, MTV and Wall Street Journal all ran pieces about this team. Yet, some questioned New York's tactics of physical play as a win at all cost approach. Their reputation grew, and the

(© Frank Schmidt)

winning continued. New York claimed five straight UPA National Championships starting in 1989 and five World Championships by the time their reign ended.

As teams from all over the world tried to knock off the kings, New York New York ended up dismantling themselves. The team decided to disband after the 1993 UPA Nationals after another victory. The team united to represent the United States for the Worlds Club Championships in 1994. New York rallied to score the last 4 points in the finals to win. After the season, new teams formed but did not perform to past New York standards. The reign was over for New York New York, but their legacy continues as champions and innovators to the sport.

Profile: Death Or Glory

Boston's Death or Glory (DoG) is the most dominant open team in ultimate history. They continued their success in 1999 with a record sixth consecutive National Championship, defeating last year's runner-up, the Santa Barbara Condors. Death or Glory's stars include Jim Parinella, Steve Mooney and Jeremy Seeger. These players are virtually unstoppable on the ultimate field who also bring mental toughness and impeccable strategy to compliment their game. DoG has been able to keep their team a

(© *Stephen Chiang*)

dominant force, adding young players such College Callahan Award Winners Fortunat Mueller and Justin Safdie; making the team a force to be dealt with for years to come.

By winning the National title in 1995, DoG qualified to be the U.S. representative at the World Ultimate Championships in Sweden in August of the following year. DoG left with the World Championship after a convincing 21-13 victory over Sweden in the final. Boston also won the Spirit of the Game Award. The last time the World Champions also won the spirit award was when Boston was last in Sweden, in 1983.

DoG is a very innovative team, successfully utilizing an array of clams and zone defenses, complemented by a wide-open and opportunistic offense. Using this run-and-gun style, DoG won both the 1994 & 1995 UPA National Championships by the largest margin of victory ever and with the highest scoring efficiency ever in U.S. finals competition. DoG has established a dynasty that may never be matched.

(© *Stephen Chiang*)

Stanford Superfly

Superfly is the women's team for Stanford University. Without fear of exaggeration, this team has been the most successful women's college team in history.

The team possesses great cohesion through practice and experience. Each year, the older players along with coaches teach younger players the basics of ultimate. The team usually has strong numbers to field two teams, which allows for new players to gain valuable experience. The transformation of the team starts in fall and leads up to College Nationals in spring. Stanford is usually in the thick of action when spring time rolls around.

The team embodies much of the fundamentals of

(© *Scobel Wiggins*)

ultimate with solid disc skills and effective defense. The team believes in 'chilly' or calm offensive strategy and to get psyched up on defense. The fundamentals and cohesion have lifted Superfly to seven national finals appearances in eight years ('95-'02). It is amazing to sustain such high quality of play on the college level. Jennifer Donnely who coached the team to three straight championships has been instrumental in creating an atmosphere of excellence for her players. Dominique Fontenette graduated from Superfly and represented the United States Ultimate Team at the 2001 World Games in Japan. She has also played with Lady Godiva and Fury.

Graduates give inspiration to the new team, and the team has no intention of letting up. Players play throughout the year in preparation for college season. Superfly has elevated the college game and wants to raise their game even higher.

Interview with Canada's Anne-Marie Carey

How did you get involved with ultimate and when?
It was in 1991, I was in Toronto, and it was the year they hosted World Clubs. I went and checked out a day of disc, got a taste of the tournament party, was handed a disc to practice with, and had decided I needed to play. I played a few games before leaving town for university, and never got to play again until the summer of 98.

What are your strengths?
My biggest strength is passion – an absolute love of the game and desire to continually grow with the sport. Confidence is another big one. In terms of on field strengths, I

am definitely a D line player. Despite Dennis Rodman being a freak, I decided to wear #91 in honor of him being my defensive guru!

What are your favorite memories?
I once hopped on a bus Friday night after work, arrived in Philadelphia 12 hours later, grabbed a cab to the fields, arriving just as the first pulls were being thrown. I knew one person at the tournament, who wasn't even on my team. Played all day, partied most of the

night, slept crammed in a living room, got up, showed up late despite a first round bye, played Sunday, was part of this college  team's first win, got a lift to the bus station and got back home with a spare hour to grab some breakfast and clean the dirt off my knees before heading straight to work. I'd do it again in a second! After play one Saturday, a carload got out at a convenience store to pick up some post-game beer, and the cashier took one look at the bunch of us and asked why I was the only one with dirt all over me. I'd just come out of playing my first men's tournament and was going extra hard and bidding all over the place. The boy's egos took a little beating that day!

Probably my best memory is Canadian Nationals in 2000. I had just moved to Vancouver, but was playing my last tournament with the women's team I'd captained in Toronto that summer. After our first game of the tournament against Prime, Leslie Calder came over and talked to me about possibly practicing with them leading up the fall series that year. I went running over to my team in incredible giddiness convinced I'd just made the big leagues!

Who do you admire (player) or like to watch play?
I don't think I was ever inspired by a female player until I saw Leslie Calder play. The woman is incredible, and my only regret is not getting out to Vancouver soon enough to

have played a season with her on Prime. There's a lot of guys I watch in awe – whether it be their throws, incredible bids or their skies, but the sheer determination, consistency and all out grit that Leslie plays with is something I aspire to.

Is there anything else you would like to share?
Never take for granted the amount of effort and time your team captains put into the team. I organized a team for one season, and it was a pretty dedicated and consuming effort for 8 months. It's easy to just show up and play, and then complain when things are a little disorganized. If things aren't quite coming together, it is probably because your teammates could use a hand.

Interview with Finland's Topi Haaramo

How *did you get involved with ultimate and when?*
My brother introduced ultimate to me in 1995. I used to play basketball at the same time, but there was something more in ultimate and since 1996 I've played only ultimate and sometimes even lived only for ultimate. I've never regretted my choice.

What are your strengths?
Mental toughness and physicality.

What are your favorite memories?
It is definitely the WUCC (Worlds Ultimate Club Champi-onships) in '99 in Scotland when our team was best ever European team finishing 2nd.

What have you learned about yourself through ultimate?
I've found new muscles that are always aching. That boundaries can be broken when there is enough will.

What have you learned about life or others through ulti-mate?
I believe my social skills and teamwork ca-pabilities have devel-oped through ultimate. After all it is teamwork all the way.   Ultimate has opened my eyes lit-tle more in the sense that there are all sorts of life walking on the earth. And that variety makes it all worth a while.   And there's nothing better than hav-ing a good time with good friends.

Do you have advice for other ultimate players?
Have fun! If you are en-joying life, the rest will follow.

What would you change about ultimate?
Some people say that ultimate should be developed so that it would be more spectator friendly and that way ultimate could grow bigger. Some suggestions (might be bit far fetched): making the game faster, adding time limits to offense, goals that are passed further than half court would give 2 points.

Who do you admire (player) or like to watch play?
I admire my brother's (Ville Haaramo) skill and will in the defense, Ilkka Rämö's sureness with the disc, Timo Vaskio's virtuosity with the disc and Tomi Bruns's power moves. All of them play in Liquidisc (isn't it natural to admire your teammates?!). I like to watch Justin Safdie (DoG), Mikael Forsgren (Skogshyddans, Sweden) and Ville Nevalainen (SOS, Finland).

What tournaments or championships have you won?
Outdoors: Finnish nationals 4 times.
Indoors: Finnish nationals 3 times, NICC 2001 (Northern Indoor Club Championships), Wintertrofen 2001 (Most respected tournament in indoors in Europe)

What are your favorite tourneys?
WUCC's and Paganello, the beach tournament in Italy, are. WUCC's I take very seriously and it is most rewarding to succeed in there. WUCC's are basically the reason why I play ultimate and practice hard. Paganello is just for fun.

Interview with Steve Mooney

How did you get involved with ultimate and when?
I learned a two finger on Foss Hill at Wesleyan University, Middletown CT in 1978. But I really got hooked over the summer of '79 playing with the Circus on Strawberry Flats in Berkeley CA. Those guys couldn't understand why I had to go back east early for soccer camp instead of Worlds at Santa Cruz. My bad... soccer is great but Santa Cruz rules.

What are your strengths?
As far back as I can remember, I have loved sports more than anything else. All sports. That love has been a driving force in my life... along with being the middle of three brothers with whom I com-

(© *Stephen Chiang*)

peted for everything day in and day out. Oh, I'm tall, reasonably fast, and I generally don't drop the disc when on O.

What are your favorite memories?
A massive Fools huck, a particular layout in the '82 finals. Driving to Mars in a rented van for the 4th of July. Playing in a packed stadium in front of 10,000 soccer fans wasn't bad either (who cares if they weren't there to see us). Getting in shape.

What have you learned about yourself through ultimate?
Sounds trite... but that life is good, and that I can't throw a two finger into the wind.

(© *Stephen Chiang*)

What have you learned about life or others through ultimate?
I wouldn't trade team sports and ultimate in for anything. They can't teach what we learn on the field in business school. They try to with the various case studies and seminars on leadership, and collaboration. But playing ultimate

is the fast track to figuring out how to work with people.

What would you change about ultimate?
The name. I like what a friend suggested: Field Disc. I have to admit that the 2 point line was exciting, even if it cost us a tournament as our opponents came back from 9-14 game to 15. OUCH!

Who do/did you admire (player) or like to watch play?
Jeremy Seeger for his grace and agility. Joey Giampino for his closing speed and incredible catches. Molly Goodwin for her focus and determination.

What tournaments or championships have you won?
I wish I really knew... UPA Nationals, Worlds, Fools East, Purple Valley, Easterns/Boston Invitational, Clambake, Mother's Day, St. Louis, Boulder.

What are your favorite tourneys?
Fools East, Nationals, Boulder, Purple Valley... and any tournament in a foreign country.

Is there anything else you would like to share?
I can still get open.

Hall of Champions
UPA National Champions-Open

Year	1st Place	2nd Place	Semi-Finalists	
1977	Condors	Penn State		
1978	Condors	Cornell		
1979	Glassboro	Condors	Mich. State	Orlando
1980	Glassboro	Aerodisc	Mich. State	Condors
1981	Condors	Knights of Nee	Sky Pilots	Hostages
1982	Rude Boys	Tunas	The Gang	Hostages
1983	Windy City	Spinoffs	Condors	Sky Pilots
1984	Tunas	Flying Circus	Windy City	Condors
1985	Flying Circus	Kaboom	Windy City	Tunas
1986	Windy City	Flying Circus	Titanic	Kaboom
1987	New York	Windy City	Titanic	Tunas
1988	Tsunami	Titanic	New York	Windy City
1989	New York	Tsunami	Titanic	Iguanas
1990	New York	Iguanas	Titanic	Windy City
1991	New York	Big Brother	Iguanas	Tsunami
1992	New York	Commonwealth	Windy City	Rhino Slam
1993	New York	Dbl Happiness	Big Brother	Rhino Slam
1994	Death or Glory	Dbl Happiness	Cojones	Chesapeake
1995	Death or Glory	Sockeye	Cojones	Dbl Happiness
1996	Death or Glory	Sockeye	Nice Guys	Chicago Z
1997	Death or Glory	Sockeye	Ring of Fire	Chicago Z
1998	Death or Glory	Condors	Ring of Fire	WSL
1999	Death or Glory	Condors	Furious George	Sub Zero
2000	Condors	Furious George	Death or Glory	Jam
2001	Condors	Jam	Death or Glory	Furious
2002	Furious George	Ring of Fire	Death or Glory	Sockeye

UPA National Champions-Women

Year	1st Place	2nd Place	Semi-finalists	
1981	B.L.U.	Synergy	Glassboro	
1982	Zulu	Fisheads	Dark Star	
1983	Fisheads	Spinsters	Dark Star	
1984	Condors	Fisheads	Andromeda	
1985	Condors	Animation	Fisheads*	
1986	Condors	Nemaheads	Safari	Smithereens
1987	Condors	Lady Godiva	Ozone	Nemesis
1988	Godiva	Smithereens	Condors	Mamba
1989	Crush Club	Lady Godiva	Satori	Maine-iacs
1990	Maine-iacs	Safari	Satori	Godiva
1991	Godiva	Maine-iacs	Satori	Condors
1992	Maine-iacs	Lady Godiva	Satori	Block Party
1993	Maine-iacs	Lady Godiva	Ozone	Swarm
1994	Felix	Ozone	Women on the Verge	Godiva
1995	Godiva	Verge	Nemesis II	Ozone
1996	Godiva	Ozone	Nemesis II	Peppers
1997	Godiva	Schwa	Nemesis	Women on the Verge
1998	Godiva	Verge	Ozone	Home Brood
1999	Fury	Schwa	Verge	Godiva
2000	Godiva	Schwa	Fury	Prime
2001	Godiva	Schwa	Fury	Prime
2002	Godiva	Fury	Riot	Ozone

College UPA National
Champions - Open

Year	1st Place	2nd Place	Semi-Finalists	
1984	Stanford	Glassboro St.	U. Mass.	U. Penn
1985	U. Penn	U. Mass	Cornell	SW Missouri
1986	U. Mass	Stanford	Cornell	UCSB
1987	Chabot C.C.	U.C. Santa Barbara	Cornell	Cal Poly SLO
1988	UC Santa Barbara	Texas	Columbia	Stanford
1989	UC Santa Barbara	Stanford	Texas	Carnegie Mellon
1990	UC Santa Barbara	UNC Wilmington	Cornell	SUNY Purchase
1991	UC Santa Cruz	UNC Wilmington	Cornell	UCSB
1992	Oregon	Cornell	UNC Wilmington	UC Berkeley
1993	U.N.C. Wilmington	U.C. Santa Barbara	UC Santa Cruz	Carleton
1994	East Carolina	Stanford	UC Santa Barbara	Carleton
1995	East Carolina	UC Santa Cruz	UNC Wilmington	Stanford
1996	UC Santa Barbara	Carleton	Wisconsin	Cornell
1997	UC Santa Barbara	Stanford	Carleton	East Carolina
1998	UC Santa Barbara	Stanford	Brown	NC State
1999	North Carolina State	UC Santa Barbara	Brown	Carleton
2000	Brown	Carleton	UC Santa Barbara	Colorado
2001	Carleton	Colorado	UC Santa Barbara	Oregon
2002	Stanford	Wisconsin	William and Mary	Carleton

College UPA National
Champions - Women

Year	1st Place	2nd Place	Semi-Finalists	
1987	Kansas	UC Davis	Humboldt State	UMass
1988	UC Santa Barbara	UC Davis	Humboldt State	Oregon
1989	UC Davis	Michigan	UC Santa Barbara	Carleton
1990	UC Santa Barbara	Michigan	Cornell	Carleton
1991	UC Santa Barbara	UC Berkeley	Cornell	Carleton
1992	UNC Wilmington	Oregon	Columbia	UC Berkeley
1993	UC Berkeley	UNC Wilmington	Humboldt State	Carleton
1994	UC Santa Cruz	UC Santa Barbara	UNC Wilmington	Indiana
1995	UC Santa Cruz	Stanford	UNC Wilmington	Colorado
1996	UNC Wilmington	Stanford	UC Berkeley	Carleton
1997	Stanford	UBC	Rutgers	Carleton
1998	Stanford	Carleton	Oregon	Yale
1999	Stanford	Carleton	Brown	Georgia
2000	Carleton	UNC Wilmington	Georgia	UC Davis
2001	Georgia	Stanford	UC San Diego	UNCW
2002	UC San Diego	Stanford	Colorado	MIT

Open Junior's UPA National Champions

Year	1st Place	2nd Place
1998	Amherst	Brooklyn Tech
1999	Brutal Grassburn, Tn	MOHO (Seattle)
2000	MOHO (Seattle)	Newton North
2001	Gruel (Paideia HS, Atlanta)	Amherst Hurricanes

Girls Juniors UPA National Champions

Year	1st Place	2nd Place
1998	Stuyvesant	Amherst
1999	Amherst	Bronx Science
2000	Amherst Varsity	Tennessee
2001	Amherst Varsity	Brutal Grassburn, Tn

(© Rick Collins)

119

Mixed UPA National Champions

Year	1st Place	2nd Place
1998	Red Fish, Blue Fish, Ca	Pira Hiku, Co
1999	Raleigh Llama, NC	Red Fish Blue Fish
2000	Spear, NC	Trigger Hippy, Mt
2001	Trigger Hippy, Mt	Blue Ridge, Va
2002	Donner Party, Ca	Hang Time, Tx

Master's UPA National Champions

Year	1st Place	2nd Place
1991	Red Menace	Club Nimeo
1992	Rude Boys	Texas Twister
1993	Beyondors	Refugees
1994	US Tampico	Slack
1995	Squash	US Tampico
1996	Windy City	Love Handlers
1997	YESSSS!	Love Handlers
1998	New York	Tempus Fugit
1999	Old & In the Way	Herniated Disc
2000	Keg Workers	Pond Scum
2001	Keg Workers	Old & In the Way
2002	Old Sag	Old & In the Way

World Champions for National Teams

Year	Open Champs	Women's Champs
1983	Rude Boys (USA)	Melting Pot (USA)
1984	Windy City (USA)	Finland
1986	Flying Circus (USA)	Lady Condors (USA)
1988	New York (USA)	Lady Condors (USA)
1990	New York (USA)	Lady Condors (USA)
1992	Sweden	Japan
1994	New York (USA)	Maine-iacs (USA)
1996	Death or Glory (USA)	Sweden
1998	Furious George (Canada)	Lady Godiva (USA)
2000	Death or Glory (USA)	Prime (Canada)

World Champions for Club Teams

Year	Open Champs	Women's Champs
1989	Philmore (USA)	Lady Condors, (USA)
1991	New York (USA)	Lady Godiva (USA)
1993	New York (USA)	Maine-iacs (USA)
1995	Double Happiness (USA)	Women on the Verge (USA)
1997	Sockeye (USA)	Women on the Verge (USA)
1999	Death or Glory (USA)	Women on the Verge (USA)
2002	Condors (USA)	Riot (USA)

European National Championships

Year	Open Champs	Women's Champs
1980	Finland	
1981	Sweden	
1982	Sweden	Finland
1985	Sweden	Sweden
1987	Sweden	Finland
1989	Sweden	Sweden
1991	Sweden	Sweden
1993	Sweden	Sweden
1995	Sweden	Sweden
1997	Finland	Finland
2001	Sweden	England

(© *Jost Armbruster*)

Glossary

air bounce: usually a backhand throw that starts low and rises caused by thumb placement and release of disc

backhand: a standard throw; right-handed player places thumb on top of disc, curls fingers underneath, extends arm to left side of body

bid: an attempt to catch or block the disc

blade: an angled throw released with the disc edge vertical

block: to knock the disc to the ground by defender causing a turnover

break the mark: a throw that is thrown over, around or through the marker's force

buttonhook: a 180 degree cut by receiver towards the disc

clam: defense strategy that relies upon poaching, clogging throwing lanes and switching covering offensive players

clamping: grasping outside edges of disc in order to make a catch

clap catch: bring palms of hands together to catch disc; often called pancake or sandwich catch

clear out: movement of offensive player to open field space for teammate to receive pass

clog: disrupting the lanes for the offensive team

counter break: a cut by receiver starting towards corner of end-zone then quickly changing direction to opposite corner of end-zone

cup: usually three defenders that surround the thrower in a zone defense, consists of two points and a middle-middle

cut: a break by the offensive receiver

123

D: defense

deeps: either an offensive player who looks for long passes or defensive player positioned far downfield in a zone or clam

dominator: an offensive strategy to advance the disc by using solely handlers in short controlled passes

dump: a short pass backwards often used to reset the stall count

flow: continuous movement of disc by offensive team down the field

force: manner in which the marker inhibits the throwing direction

force backhand: allowing throws to backhand side of field, inhibiting throws to forehand side of the field (for right-handers)

force flick: allowing thrower to throw to forehand side of the field, inhibiting throws to backhand side of the field (for right-handers)

force middle: allowing throws to the middle of the field, inhibiting throws down the line

force true sideline: allowing throws to the closest sideline of the field that the disc is on

forehand or flick: usually a two finger grip thrown similar to a sidearm pitch in baseball

front: defensive positioning on downfield receiver in which defender is between receiver and the disc

hammer: an overhead throw with a forehand grip in which the disc is released at an angle so that it flattens out and flies upside down

handler: offensive team's primary thrower

high release: a backhand throw released around or over the marker

huck: a long throw

inside-out: the rim farthest away from the body lowered so the disc curves away outward

layout: a dive to catch or block the disc

looper: a curving throw to evade defenders

mark: defensive player guarding the thrower

middle-middle: defensive player in cup between points, inhibiting throws directly down the field

midfielder: offensive player that looks to receive mid range passes

milk: action by a receiver to delay moment of catching the disc, allowing disc to float longer in order to gain more yardage

negative angle: forehand or backhand with the outside rim of disc lower than hand

on-point: marker in cup during a zone, forcing thrower towards the middle-middle and off point

off-point: defensive player in cup inhibiting swing pass across the field

outside-in: throw with outside of disc higher than hand causing a looping trajectory of the throw

pick: an illegal block by the offensive team that inhibits a defender from guarding an opposing player

pivot: thrower must maintain foot in contact with same spot on ground and turn to evade marker and find receiver

poach: a move by a defender to guard someone else's receiver

poppers: offensive players during zone that try receive and advance disc through the cup

pull: initiates play with a long throw from the defense

scoober: an upside down throw with the forehand grip and released over the opposite shoulder

scramble: switching from zone or clam defense to person to person defense

shredder break: a cut by receiver from the back of the stack towards the thrower

sky: jump and stretch high to catch the disc

stack: a line of offensive players usually down the middle of the field

stall count: The defensive player counts up to 10 while defending the offensive player

straight up: marking strategy where mark inhibits throws down the field forcing throwers to loop disc around marker

step out: a lunge by the thrower to evade the marker

swing: a cross-field pass

trap: a defensive strategy to push the disc to the sideline in order for the offensive to use less of the field.

two finger grip: index and middle finger grasping rim of disc with thumb used for forehand, hammer and scoober throws

up calls or up: what teammates shout to indicate that the disc is in the air

wings: defensive players in zone behind cup and in front of deeps

zone: a defense that utilizes cup and downfield positioning

<u>Order Form</u>

Postal Orders:
Studarus Publishing
359 Cannon Green #G
Goleta, Ca 93117
United States of America

Inquiries via Email:
studarus@conceptioncoast.org

Sales Tax:
Please add 7.75% for books shipped to
California addresses

Shipping:
$4.00 for the first book and
$2.00 for each additional book

Ship Books to:

_____

_____

_____

_____

_____

FOOTWEAR :: APPAREL :: DISCS

**Proud supporters of this book
and ultimate everywhere**